AuthorHouse™ UK Ltd.
500 Avebury Boulevard
Central Milton Keynes, MK9 2BE
www.authorhouse.co.uk
Phone: 08001974150

First published by AuthorHouse 7/20/2009

ISBN: 978-1-4389-7114-8 (sc)

This book is printed on acid-free paper.

Dedication

For Gwen, whose constant love, support and encouragement enabled Donald to have such a fruitful ministry.

Contents

List of Photographs

Foreword

What you are about to read is the story of a remarkable man. Like so many Christians who have, later, had a significant ministry he had humble beginnings and, outwardly, had no great qualifications. Yet, in those churches where Donald McCallum served, and in his wider ministry, he touched, to the glory of God, the lives of many and displayed the love of Christ, whether it was to the deprived and suffering, the overseas student, or the young people of our churches. All he did, and achieved, as 'just a wee boy', stemmed from a deep and powerful commitment to his Lord and the advancement of His Kingdom of justice and truth.

Some of us were privileged, not only to be involved in some aspects of what Donald McCallum did particularly among the young people of our churches, but also to know him as a close and valued friend. Occasionally, in the Baptist ministry, you have an ambivalent relationship to your predecessor. Donald was my predecessor in Stirling Baptist Church but it only served to deepen our relationship. The added bonus was that I became his pastor when Donald and Gwen retired to Kippen.

What follows is an moving and inspiring story, told in a straightforward way, by the daughter he loved so dearly. I warmly commend it to the reader. You will be touched by it though it could well be that the level of your own compassion for others will be challenged!

Jim Taylor.

Preface

It has given me great pleasure to write this book which began as a half promise made to Dad in the last few months of his life. During those months he spent a lot of time reminiscing about all that God had done through his ministries in four very different Scottish churches. In addition to these ministries, I had often heard him tell stories of his childhood and of his experiences in the Second World War and realised that the account of his life was both exciting and inspiring.

Others had come to the same conclusion and some of his stories, particularly those of his early life, had already been recorded. At that time I did not want to make a promise I could not keep, but I did tell him that if ever I had the time and opportunity, I would write his biography. This delighted him and I am equally delighted to have completed the task. I hope that you will enjoy the story and be thrilled at what God can do with someone who willingly gives his life over to God's purposes.

During the writing of this biography many people have written or spoken to me about Dad. I hope I have acknowledged all contributions, but if you have been missed out please forgive me. The omission was not deliberate. A number of people have been mentioned by name in this biography but, inevitably, many have been left out. Please do not be offended if your name does not appear. Once again, the omission was not deliberate.

Ruth Millican

Acknowledgements

The greatest thanks go to my family who supplied many details and checked drafts for accuracy: particular thanks to my Mum, Gwen McCallum, but also to my brother Peter McCallum, his wife Ann-Marie and my aunt Ruby Dudgeon; thanks are also due to my husband, Charles, for putting up with all the researching and writing I have done over the last two years and to the younger members of the family - Donald, Kirsty, Calum and his wife Catriona – for practical help.

For willingly writing the preface: Rev. Jim Taylor;

For interviewing Dad, typing up notes, then giving the notes and tapes to me and thus inspiring me to begin this biography: Jim Ingham;

For permission to use the Baptist Union of Scotland archives and to quote from the 'Scottish Baptist Magazine': The Baptist Union of Scotland;

For information about the early years: George and Violet Smith;

For information about the years in Islay: Alan Bell, Robert Forrest and Rev. Adam Plenderleith;

For information about the years in Granton: George and May Hogg;

For information about the years in Stirling: Glenys Jones, Betty Lauder, Jean Lewis, Linda Rodger, Islwyn and Ruth Williams;

For information about the years in Glasgow: Mabel Blues, Bill Dougall, Rev. Paul Gardiner, Margaret Innes, Marjorie McInnes, Nan Murray, John and Morag Stewart;

For information about the years of retirement: Peter Brown, Alec Craig, Donald King, Molly Parsons, Lesley Robinson and the deacons of Cornton Baptist Church, Stirling;

For carefully checking the draft copy: Catherine Fleming

Chapter 1

Childhood and teenage years

The sun was shining as the ferry approached Port Askaig on the island of Islay off the west coast of Scotland. It was June 2006 and Gwen McCallum stood on deck looking at the view, a view she knew so well.

"The sun was shining just like this on the day Donald and I first arrived on Islay sixty years ago", she remarked, "and now I am here to present the Rev. Donald P. McCallum Memorial Shield at the Islay High School prize-giving. As I look back over those sixty years I have so much for which to be thankful."

Gwen's thoughts drifted back to the many times she and Donald had reminisced about the past – Donald's childhood and teenage years, his experiences in the army during the Second World War, meeting each other in war-time Cambridge, almost fifty-five years of very happy marriage, service in four very different pastorates and the years of retirement. Donald had particularly enjoyed thinking about the ways God had led him through his life and as he reminisced there was one comment frequently on his lips:

"I am completely amazed at what God has done through an ordinary wee boy from Edinburgh."

The First World War had almost two more years to run when on 1st February 1917 a young couple, Duncan and Robina McCallum, welcomed the birth of this 'ordinary wee boy', their first child, whom they named Donald Peter. He was born in his grandmother's home, a tenement in Morningside Road, Edinburgh and grew up in the family home along with his two younger sisters – Margaret and Ruby - at Belhaven Terrace, just off Morningside Road .

Donald's mother, Robina Scott, had been born in Glasgow, but was brought up in Edinburgh after her father obtained a post as an engineer for MacKenzie and Moncur, a well known company in Edinburgh. Donald's father, Duncan, came from Campbeltown in Argyll. Like many Highland young men, he joined the army and went on to serve with the Argyll and Sutherland Highlanders. Early on in his army career he was wounded in the Boer War. At the outbreak of the First World War he was deemed too old to serve overseas and was made Regimental Quartermaster Sergeant, based at Stirling Castle. By the time of Donald's birth, however, Duncan had left the army and the young couple had settled in Edinburgh where Duncan worked as an attendant in The Royal Scottish Museum. At the end of the war, he was formally discharged from the army, having served for twenty-one years.

Donald's parents met in Edinburgh at a little mission hall, the Morningside Mission. Services were held there every Sunday, with an open air service in the evening. In the summer months there was also an open air service on a Sunday afternoon on the Blackford Hill in Edinburgh. The church was run entirely by the people in the congregation and Donald's family played their part in all the activities. His maternal grandfather was the treasurer.

Donald grew up in a devout Christian home. His earliest memories were of the times of prayer with his parents when the whole family would kneel down at the end of each day, once his father was at home after his day's work. His father would pray, followed by his mother. Prayer was a very important part of their family life. Indeed, Donald's father told him that he had prayed for Donald even before he was born. This happy Christian family life laid the foundation for Donald's own ministry.

Donald with his parents and sisters in 1923

Long before Donald became a Christian, his father took him to see a missionary film. He was inspired by this film and prayed that there would still be Christian work for him to do when he grew up.

"I was so afraid that the missionary work would be completed before I was able to play my part!" he later confessed.

From an early age, therefore, Donald knew that he wanted to go into some form of Christian work.

During Donald's childhood, tram cars ran in Edinburgh. These were cable cars, not electric cars, so they rattled their way through the streets and Donald could remember their distinctive sound for the rest of his life. The sound was particularly associated with his grandmother's home where he sometimes spent weekends. This was a special treat as he was thoroughly spoiled! From the bedroom, he could hear the cable cars rattling up and down Morningside Road.

A less happy memory was of his first experience of formal schooling. During Donald's first year at primary school, his grandfather would take him to Morningside School each day, but Donald had no intention of staying there. He regularly ran home, often arriving back at the house before his grandfather had walked back from the school. His parents were at a loss to understand the reason for Donald's unhappiness at school, and the running home continued on a regular basis throughout his first year of schooling. His parents hoped that a summer spent with his father's relatives in Campbeltown would help him to relax and feel better about school. It did go some way towards easing the situation, but it was some time before Donald was willing to stop running home.

"I cannot think why I kept running home," commented Donald in later years, "but I vividly remember arriving home even before my grandfather had walked back from the school. My mother could hardly believe I had run home so quickly."

Summer holidays were spent in Campbeltown. Donald and his sisters looked forward to their holidays, counting the days until they could go. Even the journey was exciting and adventurous for a young boy. In the 1920s Campbeltown was a very isolated place and it was difficult to get there. The family had to rise very early in the morning to catch the 6.30am train from Edinburgh to Glasgow Central. Then there was another train to Gourock where the family boarded a steamer which sailed to Lochranza and Pirnmill in Arran, across to Carradale and on to Kintyre. A small boat came out at Saddell in Kintyre to meet their steamer and then the steamer continued on to Campbeltown, arriving in the late afternoon.

Donald remembered these holidays with great delight. He often thought about the carefree Campbeltown days.

"I particularly remember going on the little train to visit relatives at Machrihanish and visits to the pier in Campbeltown when the fishing boats were in", he remarked. "My cousins and I would return home with herring strung on our shoelaces!"

There were lots of cousins in Campbeltown. Later in life, Donald often referred to the time when he and his sisters decided to count their cousins. He joked that once they reached eighty, they stopped! He did not have eighty cousins, but he certainly had a good number whose company he enjoyed during the summers of his childhood.

There were many other relatives there too. Donald was only eight when his grandfather died, but he remembered him as a native Gaelic speaker who could both read and write Gaelic. Since the 1920s, the use of Gaelic has declined in that part of Scotland and in the late 1940s Donald was visiting relatives in Campbeltown when his uncle took him to visit the last remaining native Gaelic speakers in the town.

Donald's grandfather was also noted for having the gift of second sight, although Donald was not too happy about calling it a gift and he certainly did not want it for himself for he associated it with the foretelling of disaster. A story which he often recounted concerned the time when one of his uncles on his father's side of the family was drowned off the coast of Kintyre while out fishing. Donald's grandfather was in bed when all this happened, but he 'heard' horsemen coming, even though these horsemen were too far away for him to have actually heard the horses' hoof beats. He got up and went out to meet the horsemen, knowing that something had happened, although he was not sure what had actually taken place. However, he knew something was wrong. When the men arrived they told him that his son had been drowned and they could not find the body. Donald's grandfather pointed to an area of the sea and said,

"He's down there."

The men answered, "We've been there, sir."

His grandfather replied, "Well, that's where he is."

The men went back, checked again and found the body.

When Donald was ten years old, the family moved to Saughtonhall, over on the other side of the city, not far from Corstorphine. They lived there for only a few years before moving to another part of Edinburgh, Chesser, where Donald stayed until he was married. While in Saughtonhall, the family attended a Congregational Church near where they lived, then after the move to Chesser they went to Charlotte Baptist Chapel, where his parents were baptised.

It was during his time in Chesser, at the age of sixteen, that he became a Christian. It happened one Sunday evening in Charlotte Chapel. As a young boy he had often sat in the gallery of the church with his parents and sisters, looking down on the minister in the pulpit. With a smile he confessed,

"At that time I found many of the sermons very tedious so I got into the habit of looking at the pile of sermon notes and trying to calculate how long the sermon would last!"

On this occasion, however, although he was again sitting up in the gallery, he had been thinking seriously about his relationship with God. His upbringing in a Christian family and the preaching of Dr James Scroggie in Charlotte Chapel had led him to this point. However, that night the preacher was a man named Todman Schilvers from Spurgeon's Tabernacle in London. Later in life, Donald could remember very little of that particular sermon, but at the end of the service the preacher said,

"If anyone wants to commit their lives to Christ, come and stand beside me in the pulpit." This was a very unusual request in those days and Donald's heart sank: he felt he could never do that. However, he found himself on his feet and walking up to the pulpit.

At the end of the service, the man who had founded the Scout Troop in Charlotte Chapel, known to all as Pa Evans, came up to him. He was so excited that he was trembling and he went on to tell Donald the reason for his excitement. At the beginning of the service, Charlotte Chapel was so packed that Pa Evans could find a seat only behind a pillar. He could not see the minister and, being a little deaf, he depended on both seeing and hearing the minister. Rather than being annoyed about his position, he looked round the congregation and saw Donald sitting up in the gallery. Donald had been one of his Scouts. He then said to himself,

"That's one of our boys. He doesn't come to Scouts any more. I don't know if he's a Christian. I don't think he is."

Pa Evans therefore decided that as he could not see the minister and would have problems in hearing the sermon, he would instead spend that time praying for Donald. At first he could only remember Donald's nickname, Kiltie, so he used that. Then halfway through the service he remembered his name and felt better about praying for him using his proper name. When the minister made an appeal, Pa Evans' heart sank. He thought, "This is Scotland. You don't do that kind of thing in Scotland."

Almost immediately, however, Pa Evans saw his prayer answered in a most dramatic way when Donald walked into the pulpit to commit his life to Christ. No wonder he trembled with excitement when he spoke to Donald after the service! Donald often remarked that it was Pa Evans' prayers that got him out of his seat and into the Charlotte Chapel pulpit that night. Neither of them could have even dreamed that Donald would in the future preach from that same pulpit.

Chapter 2

A developing commitment

Donald left Boroughmuir Secondary School in 1932 at the age of fifteen. He had done very well in his studies, gaining a certificate for eighth place in English while in his second year and passing all the subjects for a Higher Leaving Certificate in his final year at the school. During this time, his love of literature grew, a love which continued for the rest of his life and was clearly shown through his wide reading and the many literary illustrations in his sermons. To the end of his life he was very proud of being a former pupil of Boroughmuir and for many years wore the school scarf.

His first job, which he disliked, was in a shop which sold men's clothes. The hours were from 8.30am until 7pm for a pay of eight shillings a week. Donald had thought he was going to earn ten shillings a week, so was very disappointed! Fortunately for him, he was in that job only for a couple of months.

Donald's second job came through a contact in the Morningside Mission. George Horne was a friend of his father and the lay minister of the Morningside Mission. His weekday employment as a commercial traveller meant that he had contacts with some of the shipping companies in Leith. He heard that there was a possible job for Donald in one of these companies and informed the family.

This second job was much more to Donald's tastes – a clerk in the office of the Gibson Rankin Line at Leith Docks. Donald thoroughly enjoyed this job and served his apprenticeship there, working in the cash customs department for a long time. He lived about five miles away and had to be at work as early as 6am on a Monday morning. The reason for the early start was that perishable goods would be arriving at the dock. These goods had to pass through customs and then arrive in the shops while still fresh. Donald and his colleagues had to turn up at work early to prepare customs papers so the goods could pass through customs and be taken off to the market in good time.

When Donald started working for the Gibson Rankin Line he was fifteen and earned three pounds a month, a lot more than the eight shillings a week in his first job. His mother was delighted and was heard to remark,

"Donald's got a good job."

When he left the firm at the age of twenty he was earning five pounds a month.

There was a one-off perk to this job which Donald particularly appreciated: once he had been in the office for a year or two he was allowed a few trips on one of the firm's boats. As a result of this, at the age of seventeen, he was able to sail to Dunkirk, Antwerp and Gwent, a tremendous adventure for a young man in the 1930s. He loved the excitement of these trips, enjoying going ashore to explore for himself. Particularly memorable was the trip to Antwerp where he explored the town, using his schoolboy French to help him on his way. He knew nothing about the town and had only a smattering of the language, but enjoyed a wonderful time of exploration before returning to the boat for the homeward journey.

The only expense incurred on such an expedition was a shilling for each meal consumed while on the journey. Early on in the voyage, Donald ate his meals with the crew, but the captain of the boat looked at him and remarked,

"I don't think we will see much of you on this journey."

He was right: the boat was barely past the Bass Rock when Donald was sick. Despite the seasickness, Donald thought the trip was worth every minute. Since he was sick so much, he did not have to pay for many meals which, as he later remarked, kept his expenses down – which was more than could be said for anything else!

After being in the shipping office for five years, Donald went on to work in a builders' merchant's office – Hendersons, in York Place. This was a step up for him and after a while in this job he was earning four pounds a week. However, it was while in this office that he had a real test of his Christian lifestyle. One day a customer wanted to see the boss. The boss, however, was busy and told Donald to say that he was not in the office. Donald said,

"But you are in the office!"

and another lad was sent to do the job. Donald was always sure that his honest reply had cost him promotion, because when the next opportunity came along the other lad was given promotion and Donald was passed over.

This incident, however, clearly showed where Donald's priorities lay. After making a public Christian commitment, he threw himself wholeheartedly into Christian service. At the time of Donald's conversion, Charlotte Chapel had started an extension work in the Stenhouse area of Edinburgh. A church was built there and Donald, his parents and his sister Margaret decided that they would give this church their support. Donald did open air work with his father which gave him an opportunity to do some speaking. He was baptised in the Stenhouse church and was then elected as a deacon (a leader) in the church when he was still a teenager. He also became a Sunday School teacher and started a Bible Class, looking after a class of ten year old boys when he himself was only seventeen.

In addition to this, he began a group called the Covenanters for teenage boys, some of them not much younger than himself. Some of these boys were quite wild, but Donald ran the class for several years and got to know the boys very well, visiting them in their homes and getting to know quite a number of their parents. He loved these young people and spent all his spare time with them, taking them for walks and going on outings to Canty Bay, near North Berwick, a permanent campsite for the 6th Waverley Charlotte Chapel Scouts, purchased for the troop by Pa Evans. Sometimes he would go straight from work to whatever he was doing with the boys, not even returning home for a meal first. Working with these boys was his life and he threw himself wholeheartedly into the task, so much so that his mother remarked,

"Donald is a household name in Stenhouse."

His pastoral skills were developed as he spent time

with the boys and visited their homes, instinctively realising that the gift of his time was invaluable. Donald became so well known in the area that when he was speaking at open air services, the windows of the houses would be opened so that people could listen to him.

Along with the developing ministry among these boys, Donald's burning ambition was to go to China as a missionary. The wife of one of the ministers of Stenhouse Baptist Church was an ex-China missionary and she took him along to some CIM (China Inland Mission) meetings and prayer meetings. As a result, Donald became very interested in the Mission and read as much as he could about their work. He wanted very much to go to China and was sure that he had told the Lord often enough for Him to get the message!

He began to prepare himself for going to China. A friend of the family who worked with the Edinburgh Medical Missionary Society (EMMS) told Donald that there would be an opportunity to take part in some of their work, if he was willing. Donald thought he would have a go, because any skills he could pick up might come in useful on the mission field. Eventually he was going there twice a week. He joined medical students who were intending to go to the mission field when their training was over, put on a white jacket and followed the doctors around. Soon he found that he was able to give basic treatment, such as putting on dressings. He enjoyed doing this for he felt he was helping people and this gave him great satisfaction.

There was a dental clinic twice a week. Two dentists came, one on a Tuesday and one on a Friday, giving their services free. The people who came to EMMS for dental treatment did not therefore have to pay large fees – only two shillings for extractions. After watching the medical students go in to the clinic, Donald decided that he too would go in to see what was happening. He was fascinated. While the students were taught how to extract teeth, Donald stood at the back watching, not wanting to assert himself in case he was asked to do something and made a mistake. He was, however, dressed in the same way as the rest of the students.

Patients at the clinic were given a primitive form of gas. The anaesthetic was given with the aid of a tin mug full of boiling water and a test tube attached to a mask. The test tube was filled with a chemical which then evaporated and formed a gas. The gas went through the tube and the patient inhaled it, rendering him unconscious for about two minutes. The dentist then had to work hard and work fast, so that the teeth were extracted before the patient came round.

On one occasion, the dentist approached Donald and asked,

"Would you take this one out?"

Donald thought that the dentist was trying to get rid of him by asking him to take a patient out of the room, so he answered,

"Yes."

It was only when the dentist walked away to supervise the anaesthetising that Donald realised that he had been asked to remove the patient's tooth! He decided to give it a try, so the dentist showed him what to do and he followed suit. After that, he was in the dental clinic every week.

At that time, in the 1930s, there was a great deal of

unemployment and poverty. One of Donald's friends was unemployed. He had terrible toothache, but could not afford to go to the dentist, so Donald told him to come down to the clinic. Once his friend was at the clinic and anaesthetised, Donald explained to the dentist that this man was his friend and asked the dentist to be good to him.

"Right, you do it!"

the dentist replied, so Donald took out his friend's teeth and, much to his relief, the friend was none the worse for the experience.

While Donald was preparing himself for the mission field, the world was changing. At the beginning of the Second World War in 1939 Donald was twenty-two. During the war years he was to realise that God had been preparing him for a kind of service he could never have anticipated.

Chapter 3

The War Years: North Africa and Sicily

War was declared in 1939 and on 18th January 1940, just before his twenty-third birthday, Donald was called up. Before the call up papers arrived, Donald had talked with his father about his reluctance to use a gun and kill people.

"I couldn't possibly kill people", he said. "How can I in all conscience join the army where I will be expected to kill?"

His father's reply settled the matter for him. "By joining the army you will be protecting your mother and your two sisters."

This convinced Donald that it was right for him to join up. In spite of his reluctance to use a gun, he did not become a conscientious objector because he felt he had to protect his family and the Nazi advance had to be stopped. He had to play his part in the war.

When called up for interview, Donald was first of all asked what he did as a job. He explained that he had trained as a clerk in a shipping office and currently worked in a builders' merchant's office. Questions then led on to his hobbies and Donald explained that he was very involved in the work of his church and also in the work of the Edinburgh Medical Missionary Society where his involvement was in dental and medical work. The result of this interview was that he was placed in the Medical Corps with the 51st Highland Division of the Eighth Army, when it was reconstituted after the fall of France. Although he had to learn how to use a gun for defence, he would not be expected to kill and this made him realise that his work with the Edinburgh Medical Missionary Society had been part of God's plan for his life, for without this experience he would certainly have been drafted into the infantry.

Donald wrote an article about his war experiences, so let him tell this part of the tale himself:

"For the first two years our wanderings were confined to this country, preparing for the day of action which never seemed to come. We lived in a factory, village halls and Nissen huts and soon forgot what a comfortable bed was like. We learned to rise early, shave in cold water, and jump to it when we were told. The sergeant major, though small in stature, loomed large on our horizon and we feared him as we never feared the enemy!"

When Donald joined the Royal Army Medical Corps (RAMC), they were unarmed. They were, however, trained in self defence, should it become necessary, so he was taught how to shoot and how to fire a grenade at a tank. Donald made it as clear as he could that he had no intention of killing anybody, firmly stating,

"I cannot kill people and try to cure them at the same time."

During the years of war, he was often with the infantry when the only weapon he had was a stretcher to carry off the men who had been hit.

When Donald went into the army, he resolved that he would make his Christian commitment clear from day one. He knew he would have to do this, so on the first night he knelt down at his bedside and prayed. He did this quite deliberately, but later admitted that he did not do much praying that night! However, he was sure that he had to make his witness somehow and he had to do it openly. It was not long before everybody knew of his Christian commitment and Donald felt that it was important for him to behave in a Christian way as well as to witness to his beliefs. As testimony to this, a fellow soldier, who remained a close friend after the war, said that Donald had never put a foot wrong in the army and that his life matched his Christian commitment.

Christian fellowship was important from the very beginning. Again, let Donald recount the story himself:

"It all started on 18th January 1940 when I found myself with many other men in the Dunblane Hydro awaiting the sorting out into our respective units. I had met a Christian fellow with whom I used to work and was speaking to him when someone approached us with the words, "Are youse Christians?" We said that we were and so the fellowship that was to mean so much to us began to take shape."

On 11th June 1942 Donald and about 4000 of his fellow soldiers sailed from Liverpool on the 'Duchess of Richmond', destination unknown. Two months later they landed in Egypt after a short stopover in Capetown. By then the Christian fellowship among the troops had become well established:

"The Christian men got together and, with the help of a Christian officer who led us – Captain David Milnes – obtained the use of the hospital and later one of the holds

as a meeting place. We read, prayed, and studied the Bible together and on four occasions partook of the Lord's Supper. We obtained a copy of a tract and had it reprinted at Capetown and used it for distribution among the troops.

Last of all we held a great meeting in one of the dining rooms of the ship, chaired by the Captain, also a Christian, and at which our Christian officer preached the gospel and made an appeal. We printed a souvenir of our fellowship on the ship's printing press and called it the Convoy Crusader."

Until his death in July 2001, Donald kept – and treasured – a copy of the Convoy Crusader. David Milnes was wounded in the eye at Alamein and won the Military Cross for his courage.

Arriving in Egypt, Donald and his fellow soldiers landed at the port of Tufik and eventually went up to the desert to the Alamein Line which the 8th Army was holding. Donald, along with his fellow soldiers, found time to marvel at the countryside: donkeys, camels, cars and trams in the streets of Cairo; the wonderful sight of the pyramids rising out of the desert; arriving in the Nile valley after crossing the desert and being amazed at the line of dark olive-green country which marked the passage of the Nile. In addition to this, Donald met some Egyptian Christians and worshipped with them in a little church which had been made out of aeroplane packing cases. Donald long remembered the radiant face of one Egyptian Christian with whom he shared fellowship later that day.

Egypt, with the contrast of the desert and the lush Nile valley fascinated Donald.

"The desert in these days was as busy as any city.

Tracks led here and there and along them travelled troops, tanks, armoured cars, ambulances and lorries. Only one road, the coast road, travelled across this desert land and it stretched far to the west of Tripoli – the capital of Italian Africa – and although we did not think it, in a few months of fighting and travelling we were to be there."

The battle of Alamein began on 23rd October 1942 and lasted into November. Ten thousand men lost their lives. The German army was broken and retreated to Tunis. Donald was running the unit canteen at Alamein so was not actually involved in the battle itself, but for the rest of his life he remembered the sound of eight hundred guns going off at once. The Axis armies began their long retreat and the 8th Army's long advance across the desert began – past Sollum Hellfire Pass, up to the escarpment and the Libyan desert, stopping outside Torbruk, and then cutting across the desert to El Agheile on the Gulf of Sirte south of Benghasi. Christmas 1942 was spent there. The area around El Agheile was heavily mined and the Medical Corps was kept busy with casualties.

Soon after joining the army, Donald had been sent on a bomb and mine course to learn how to defuse bombs in preparation for being sent into action. As a result of this he was reckoned to be the bomb and mine expert in his unit. On one occasion in the desert some of the infantry had been caught in a tank trap, so Donald and some other soldiers were sent to dig some graves and bury them. One of Donald's friends went over to what he thought was a body, then shouted,

"It's only a camel!"

Almost immediately there was a bang as he stood on a mine. The NCO in charge said,

"I'd like you to haul him out."

Donald took his bayonet and went over to his friend's body, prodding every foot of ground as he went. Once back on safe ground they buried his friend as well as the men who had been caught in the tank trap.

As the German army moved on, the British army moved after them. Donald's unit was part of a group which made a dash for the city of Misurata which they reached without too much trouble. A battle was fought near Homs and in early 1943 the 8th Army reached Tripoli. Churchill reviewed the victory parade in Tripoli.

Donald was impressed by Tripoli – its people, shops, lemon groves and vegetation, describing an oasis of rest and enjoyment for desert-weary troops. He was also given the opportunity to visit Leptis Magna – the great North African seaport of Ancient Roman days – about 70 miles east of Tripoli.

It was well worth the long journey to see the pillars, the streets and the buildings of a city that flourished in ancient times. For centuries the sand had covered it and by 1943 the Italians had excavated only part of it.

After Tripoli, the army pushed into Tunisia and had a pleasant few days near a seaside village, Bon Grara, opposite the island of Djerba. There Donald enjoyed the experience of drinking tea with some Arab men – tea made strong, sweet and without milk and served in a small receptacle as a delicacy.

While Donald was in Tunisia he was attached to the 2nd Battalion of the Seaforth Highlanders. At one point they walked into battle with the artillery opening up behind them, firing over their heads. Some men fell, so Donald began to pick them up. Prisoners of war were passing by, so Donald made two of them stretcher bearers to carry the wounded back to the first medical post. By the time he had done this, his unit had moved on. Donald set off across the battlefield to find his unit, eventually coming across the Black Watch, and asked their officer if he knew where the Seaforths were. Two of Donald's fellow soldiers from the Seaforth Highlanders were working with the Black Watch and when they saw him they asked if he would say a prayer over one man who had just been killed. In the middle of the battlefield, Donald stood holding his tin hat over his head, saying a prayer over the body of this man who had just been killed. Many years later Donald remarked,

"I took many funerals during my life, but never again one in quite those circumstances."

By early summer, the 8th Army had made contact with the British 1st Army and with the Americans. Just before the Tunisian battle ended, Donald and his fellow soldiers found themselves on the move again. This time they were moving east and many of them thought joyfully that they were on their way home. However, this was not to be. Another campaign was in the offing and Donald's division was to be specially trained in Algeria. The journey over the Atlas Mountains into Algeria was unforgettable. The roads seemed to cling to the sides of the mountains like snakes holding their necks up. The vehicles in which the soldiers crossed these mountains had come two thousand miles from Egypt, fighting all the way, so they were in quite a state, even although the engineers had done their best to maintain them. One of their officers was a bit nervous. He said to his driver,

"Put your brakes on, driver!"

The driver replied, "It ain't got no brakes, Sir!"

This was true: the only way to slow down was to work his way down through the gears.

Algeria was a rest for the troops after all they had been through, but they were there for only a few months. In July 1943 they were taken back to Tunisia by ship, landing at the ports of Sfax and Sousse. Once there, they were put on tank landing ships, destination unknown.

"We all had our guesses, but not until we were at sea did we learn that we were part of an invasion fleet making for the shores of Sicily. We sailed through a frightful storm – and I spent the night asleep on a coil of rope on the deck: nothing would have persuaded me to go below! But the morning broke fine and clear and the Sicilian coast seemed quiet and peaceful. And so it was – real resistance on our sector did not begin until the troops had penetrated inland. And so we landed without incident the next day."

Further inland it was a different story as the troops met strong resistance from the Herman Goering division of the German army.

The Sicilian campaign, however, was over by November 1943. Donald then had time to appreciate the beauty of the countryside, such a contrast to the North African desert, and made friends with several Sicilian people. The women began to make celebration banners to sell to the troops. The embroidered work had brightly coloured thread stitched into dark cloth, speaking of the Highland Division and their battles in North Africa. Donald bought two of these banners and treasured them.

While in Sicily, Charlie Chirnside joined the unit and was sent to drive Donald's ambulance. He was a Christian whose home was not far from Donald's in Edinburgh and Donald was sure that those in authority realised that the two men would have much in common, so put them together. They became firm friends, a friendship which lasted for the rest of their lives. Donald found him a source of encouragement for his Christian life:

"What my spiritual life owes to him I could not tell. His life of prayer and consistent Bible reading rebuked my laxness and brought me to personal revival."

Donald and Charlie were often with their own unit, the field ambulances, but they were also often attached to the Seaforths who were a fighting battalion, fighting on the front line. They asked to go with the Seaforths as they liked being with the men who were on the front line, even although it seemed such a crazy thing to do.

In November, Donald's unit headed home.

"We sailed from Sicily on Armistice Day 1943, and from Syracuse, mentioned by Luke in Acts. I read that passage as we sailed away. My last memory of Sicily is of Etna, visible long after the shores of Sicily were invisible, its snow cap floating on the clouds."

Donald (right) and Charlie beside their ambulance

Chapter 4

The War Years: Britain and Europe

It was good to be home. The troop ship sailed up the River Clyde and Donald was so happy to see the white houses and the green grass of Scotland. He was so looking forward to seeing his family again that he felt like walking home from the Clyde to Edinburgh. However, the soldiers were moved from the ship to waiting trains and he had to restrain the urge to walk home! Instead, he found himself heading for St Albans in the south of England to be trained for the second front which was to be opened in Europe.

Montgomery who had commanded the 8th Army in North Africa had been appointed to command the second front and he chose to take with him the two divisions which had served him so well in North Africa: the 51st Highland Division of which Donald was a member and the 50th Division, the Geordies. The two divisions were therefore sent immediately to their training ground, St Albans.

Not long after being sent to St Albans, the soldiers received their disembarkation leave. Many of them, including Donald, had not been home for over two and a half years and in that time there had been a number of changes in Donald's home circumstances: both of Donald's sisters had married and his father had died. However, he was delighted to be home for a while and his family was so pleased to see him safe and well.

On the way back to St Albans at the end of his leave, Donald spent some time in prayer. His time in the army had deepened his commitment to God and he prayed about his future. On this occasion Donald prayed that if God wanted him to be married He would lead him to the person of His choice. However, as he prayed he had no idea that the answer would come so very quickly! Later he commented,

"I think the Lord must have been thinking like my mother: it was about time that I was getting a move on and finding a girlfriend!"

Soon after this, Donald was asked if he would like to go to Cambridge to work in a hospital and gain a qualification which would be useful to him later on. Donald was pleased to accept the offer as he would have done anything rather than the mundane tasks in the army camp.

He was sent to Cambridge, along with another soldier named Peter Spiers. They were told to go to Addenbrooke's hospital where they would be expected to learn as much as possible and be as helpful as they could. When they arrived they were sent up to the ward where they would be working. As they reached the ward they were greeted by a charming young staff nurse who immediately asked them if they would like a cup of coffee. Needless to say, their reply was,

"Yes please!"

Donald was immediately attracted to this young nurse, Gwendoline Cripps, and fell in love with her there and then! Speaking to his close friend, Charlie Chirnside, he said,

"Charlie, I'm sure that Gwen is a Christian because she is so good to the patients. She just enjoys looking after people and is so kind and considerate even to a really crotchety old character in the ward. Only Christian grace could help her deal with that old character."

Donald was sure that such a pretty, charming girl must be engaged or married and soon noticed that Gwen was wearing a ring. He immediately thought that it was an engagement ring and that therefore Gwen could not be the right girl for him. However, a closer look made him realise that the ring was not on the engagement finger. Gwen was neither engaged nor married! It was not long before Donald found out that not only was Gwen a Christian, she was also a Baptist! They had so much in common and he felt that this was really marvellous.

Gwen was also attracted to the young soldier and realised immediately that he was a Christian. They started going out together when time permitted, but it was not easy. Gwen worked long hours as a nurse, with very little time off, and Donald was kept busy with army duties. However, they were able to enjoy some time together walking around Cambridge and boating on the Cam. From the very start, Gwen knew that Donald was the man she would marry.

Donald wrote home to let his mother and sisters know that he had a girlfriend. Needless to say, they were delighted and wanted to know all about Gwen. This was the first time Donald had shown any interest in girls, so his sister Ruby composed a poem for him which included the words, 'How have the mighty fallen!'

As well as courting Gwen, Donald enjoyed the work at Addenbrooke's hospital. He had the opportunity to go into theatre and see what happened there. Also, there were soldiers with war wounds in the hospital and he was able to help look after these men. After a few months, however, Donald's unit moved to West Ratting, a village about twelve miles from Cambridge and the men were told that they could go only six miles from the village as they would be leaving in the near future and had to be able to move on at a moment's notice . This was a blow as it meant that Donald could not go into Cambridge before he left. Some men were willing to risk going further than the six miles, but Donald felt it would be a disgrace to be away and unable to be found when he was needed.

This situation continued for six weeks. On 5th June 1944 the men were paraded and told that they would be moving off that night. Although they did not know it, D-Day was to be the next day, 6th June 1944. While Donald was being given instructions about the impending move, Peter Spiers – the man who had gone with him to Addenbrooke's hospital – ran up and said,

"Do you know who is at the gate?"

"No", replied Donald.

"It's Gwen!" Peter announced.

It was one of Gwen's rare days off and she had ridden her bicycle out to the camp in the hope of seeing Donald.

The authorities knew that Donald would not decamp, so they allowed him to borrow a bike and the two of them were able to have a couple of hours together before Donald left for occupied France. After cycling for a while, they stood up against a circle of trees and talked. Everything was uncertain and they could not be sure that they would see each other again, but they agreed to write to each other. They wrote throughout the European campaign and got to know each other better through this correspondence. Before leaving, Donald asked Gwen for a photo of herself and he kept it in his ambulance throughout the European campaign.

"Apart from reminding me of Gwen it gave the wounded soldiers a pretty face to look at!" Donald remarked.

Gwen must have been one of the first civilians to realise that the troops were about to be moved, but neither she nor Donald realised where the troops were going. Had she come to the camp one day later, the troops would have been gone. Her visit meant a great deal to Donald, for it confirmed to him that if God wanted him to be married, Gwen was the girl for him. He saw her visit not as a coincidence but as a 'God-incidence'.

That same evening, Donald set off for the south coast of England. The Allies invaded mainland Europe on D-Day, 6th June 1944, with Donald's unit reaching the Normandy coast five days later. The following days were confusing, but some memories remained.

"I remember the green fields and pretty villages – some shattered by war. I remember the River Orne and the area around Caen and passing through the outskirts of that battered town itself. I remember a little French boy in khaki who seemed to be without parents – orphaned by the war and typical of many."

After France, the troops moved on to Belgium, passing through Brussels before staying in the town of Tremeloo. The Belgians were very hospitable and made the soldiers very welcome.

The army then moved into Holland, to Eindhoven and to Nijmegen on the Waal where Donald made friends with some children and then with their parents. Some of the Dutch children had never seen chocolate, so the troops often shared their ration with them. In Enshede, near the German border, Donald and some of his friends attended a Dutch Salvation Army liberation meeting where there were two sermons and two offerings and they sang 'God save the King' for the visiting soldiers! A Dutch family in Geffin showed them the little hole in which they had hidden the radio with which they listened to London and told of the 'onerdijkers' – the men who spent their nights in the fields to avoid forced labour in Germany.

After Holland, Donald's unit moved into Germany,

". . fighting through the Reichswold forest – advancing toward the town of Goch – crossing the Rhine after and in conjunction with an invasion from the air of paratroops and glider troops based in Britain After that the war was virtually over although the fighting had not ceased. And when it did we all gave thanks."

Throughout the months and years of fighting, Donald was very aware of God's protection. On one occasion in the European campaign, Donald's unit moved into a village, at first unaware that the sun was shining on the windscreens of their vehicles. By the time the commanding officer saw what was happening, the troops were being attacked. In no time at all there were wounded men and the ambulance was full. They had to pass a crossroads which was being shelled, and just as they reached the crossroads a shell dropped on it. They continued to fill the ambulance with even more wounded men and, as they were doing this, another shell hit the crossroads. Donald stood behind the ambulance, covering his head with his arm and just hoping and praying that they would not be hit. Afterwards, Charlie, Donald's ambulance driver, found a bit of shrapnel in the driver's seat. He had been helping Donald load up the ambulance with the injured when the shrapnel had landed.

Once the fighting was over, Donald's unit was broken up, but the men were given a certain amount of choice over where they would go next. Donald asked to be sent to Berlin and found himself working in the 84th B. General Hospital, Spandau. While there he worshipped in a Baptist Church , visited the home of some German Christians in the Russian sector of Berlin, enjoyed the fellowship of the Army Scripture Reader and his group and travelled to the Hartz Mountains to a course for men preparing for the Baptist ministry which was held in the home of Von Cramm, the tennis player.

Donald's memories of Berlin were mixed. It grieved him to see the broken city, displaced people, hunger and the black market. However the memories of Christian fellowship were precious.

"I think with joy of the fellowship in Christ which I experienced when I worshipped in the Baptist Church and was welcomed by the pastor as 'our dear English brother'.

My sweetest memory is of a little communion service held in the home of a German Christian family on the night before I left for home. I still have the glass out of which I drank the wine and the wooden platter upon which lay the broken bread. The broken, bleeding Christ for a broken, bleeding world."

The glass, unfortunately, is no longer intact, but Gwen still has – and treasures – the wooden platter.

The communion plate from Berlin

In January 1946 Donald was demobilised. He was a civilian again, but the war had changed him. He had seen the terrible tragedy of war. Nevertheless, throughout the hostilities his ambulance had been a sanctuary where the Church met for worship and witness and there was a very real sense of oneness in Christ. The years ahead would bring their own joys and sorrows, but the war years had strengthened Donald's faith in Christ and increased his desire to go into full time Christian ministry. First of all, however, he looked forward to meeting Gwen again.

Chapter 5

Preparing for a new way of life

By the time Donald returned from Europe, Gwen was doing midwifery nursing in Birmingham where she had grown up, the daughter of John Ivory Cripps and Edith Jarvis. John Ivory Cripps was a Baptist minister whose first church had been Swindon Baptist Tabernacle where he had met and married Edith. Four children were born to them – Margaret, Arthur, Helen and then Gwendoline – before they moved to Birmingham where John Ivory became the minister of the Church of the Redeemer Baptist Church. Gwen was baptised in this church when she was fifteen although by that time her father was no longer the minister but had become the General Superintendent of the Baptist Churches in the West Midlands area of England.

Sadly, Gwen was only twelve when her mother died of cancer. After completing her schooling at Hansworth Grammar School, Gwen did children's nursing at Birmingham's Children's Hospital, before moving to Cambridge to do General Nursing and then back to Birmingham to do midwifery. She had always wanted to be a nurse and applied for nursing as soon as she was old enough to be accepted.

With the end of the war and Donald a civilian again, it became possible for Donald and Gwen to see more of each other. Gwen went to Edinburgh to meet Donald's family where she was very warmly and kindly received. Gwen, however, had to learn a few things about Scottish life. When first told she would be going with Donald's sisters for 'the messages', Gwen could not understand why she was then taken to the shops. To her, messages were written on paper and had nothing to do with shopping!

During her visit to Scotland, Donald took Gwen to see Loch Lomond and also took her to Stenhouse Baptist Church which she thought was wonderful. He introduced her to his friends in the church. George Smith, the son of the Sunday School Superintendent in the church, commented,

"When Donald came home on leave he visited our home regularly and brought his girl friend and later fiancée with him. Gwen impressed me as a beautiful young lady."

It was not long before Donald and Gwen were engaged and it was time to plan for the wedding and for their future lives together.

Although both Donald and Gwen were interested in missionary service in China, as they discussed their future together it became obvious to them both that they would have to begin their married lives much nearer home. Donald was very close to his mother who was a chronic asthmatic and had never had good health. Now that she was a widow he felt that he had to look after her and so their plans would have to take this into consideration. He was convinced that this was the correct course of action when some words from the first letter of Timothy, in chapter 5 verse 8, hit home to him as he read his Bible: 'The man that cares not for his own, especially his own family, is worse than a pagan.' Donald felt that God had made the point very clearly!

During the war years, the minister of Charlotte Baptist Chapel in Edinburgh, Sidlow Baxter, had taken an interest in Donald. One of Donald's sisters was friendly with one of Sidlow Baxter's daughters and through this connection he visited Donald when home on leave and prayed for him as one of the Charlotte Chapel soldiers, although Donald was a member of Stenhouse Baptist Church. On one occasion Sidlow Baxter said to him,

"Donald, when you come out of the army, if you have a problem about what you're going to do with your Christian life or with your service, don't forget that I will be willing to help you. Just let me know."

During the last leave from Berlin before Donald was demobbed, he was pondering the future and thought,

"Here I am; I have a sense of call to preach the gospel and have always felt that I would be going to China. Until now it has never occurred to me that I might preach the gospel anywhere else. I need to stay in Scotland to look after my mother, so what should I do?"

He then remembered Sidlow Baxter's words and phoned to see if he could have ten minutes to speak to him about what he would do after leaving the army.

The reply was immediate:

"I'll give you more than ten minutes! Come and see me."

Donald went to see him and explained that he was now twenty-nine, he had met Gwen and they wanted to be married. However, the responsibility for his mother was a pressing one. He therefore needed some form of service that would allow him to fulfil his duty of responsibility to his mother.

After some discussion, Sidlow Baxter's advice was,

"Write to Dr Scott, the Secretary of the Baptist Union of Scotland, and ask him to consider you as a candidate for the Home Ministry. If Dr Scott agrees and accepts you as a candidate, you can become a minister in one of the Home Missionary Churches and you will have a manse. You can marry Gwen and you can take your mother to live with you."

Donald realised that this was good advice, so he applied to Dr Scott. The Home Mission was a name given by the Baptist Union of Scotland to churches which the Union supported in the highlands and islands. All these churches were small and unable to support themselves financially, relying on the larger mainland churches within the Baptist Union of Scotland for such support.

Meanwhile, once Donald and Gwen were engaged, Gwen moved to Edinburgh to continue her nursing at the Eastern General Hospital and lived in the nurses' home. Donald was demobbed and returned to his old job in the builders' merchant's office. He had only just started the job when he received a letter from Dr Scott stating that if he was willing to go to Bowmore on the island of Islay and preach in the Baptist Church, he would, if he were willing, be considered as a candidate for ministry in that church.

Donald agreed to go and duly preached in the church. After the service, one of the deacons asked,

"If we ask you to come, will you come?"

This was an important question, for in those days the

Scottish islands were very isolated, with a basic lifestyle, very different from the cities: no gas, no electricity, cuts of peat for fuel, very little public transport on the island and infrequent ferries to and from the mainland. Donald, however, told the deacon that if they did ask him to be minister, he would come.

When Donald returned to Edinburgh he was summoned to appear before the Ministerial Recognition Committee to decide whether or not he was a fit person to be sent as a minister to anywhere, something which should have happened before he went to Islay to preach. He found this a daunting experience. As he sat down at the table with the members of the committee he thought,

"How will I survive this?"

However, the committee members turned out to be very kind and passed him as fit to serve in one of the Baptist Churches in Scotland. One of them, a wounded ex-serviceman from World War One, suggested,

"Mr McCallum, you've just come out of the army and you can get a war service grant and go to college. My advice to you, strong advice, is that you see the principal of our college and see if that is a possibility. I think you should certainly consider it."

Donald thought the advice was good and agreed to see the principal of the college. He took Gwen with him so that they could consider the matter together and also because the principal knew Gwen's father as the General Superintendent of the Baptist Churches in the West Midlands area. After some discussion, the principal explained that if Donald were to choose the college option he would have to go before the college committee and he could not anticipate what their decision might be.

Donald and Gwen went away from the meeting to talk and pray about what Donald should do. They came to the conclusion that God certainly wanted Donald in the ministry and that two doors were open to them. One – the church in Bowmore – was definitely open; they did not know if the other door – the college – would open or not. Donald had promised the deacon on Islay that he would go if the church called him as their minister. The church did call him, so in August 1946 Donald and Gwen set off for Islay.

First of all, however, there was the wedding on 17th July 1946. Gwen's family came to Edinburgh for the ceremony which took place in Charlotte Baptist Chapel and was conducted by Rev. Sidlow Baxter. Gwen's father gave her away, Charlie Chirnside (Donald's close friend from the army) was best man and Joan Field (a friend of Gwen's who had gone through all the nursing training with her) was bridesmaid. The wedding reception was held in the Chimes Hotel. Although the war had ended a year previously, to the disappointment of the families the meal was very much a wartime affair, with small portions of rather weary looking food. The wedding cake, however, was a triumph. In spite of dried fruit and eggs still being rationed, Donald's Aunt Jean, who was the buyer for MacVitties Guest (a well-known baker's shop in Princes Street, Edinburgh), had managed to provide a truly beautiful cake. The day was a very happy one for both families, with Donald and Gwen so obviously in love with each other and so well suited. In those days, photographers did not come to weddings; instead, couples had to book a time at the photographer's shop. It was all very formal, but Donald and Gwen had photographs taken before going off to Aberdeen for their honeymoon.

Donald and Gwen on their wedding day

During their time in Aberdeen, they attended the church where Willie Still, well-known in the Church of Scotland, was minister. They also met up with a friend who had been through the war with Donald. After a week there, they went down south to Birmingham and visited Gwen's family in Wiltshire. As soon as the honeymoon was over, they briefly returned to Edinburgh and almost immediately set off for Islay.

The journey to Islay was a long one. Donald and Gwen first of all took the tram into the centre of Edinburgh where they caught a train to Glasgow. Once in Glasgow, they took another train to Wemyss Bay on the Clyde coast where their sea journey started. The steamer sailed from Wemyss Bay to East Loch Tarbert at the head of the Mull of Kintyre, stopping at many places on the way. At East Loch Tarbert a bus took them to West Loch Tarbert for the steamer to Islay which first of all called in at the island of Gigha and then at the village of Craighouse on the island of Jura before arriving at Port Askaig on Islay. The sun was shining on the cliffs at Port Askaig as the boat tied up at the pier, a fine welcome for the young couple as they began the final stage of their journey - a bus from Port Askaig to Bowmore. At last they had arrived!

Chapter 6

Bowmore: an island ministry

Donald and Gwen loved Islay from the start and soon began to settle into their new home above the Baptist Church in Bowmore. It was a very different lifestyle, but they enjoyed the challenge. The day to day running of the home occupied much of Gwen's time. There was no gas or electricity so Gwen had to do all her baking in an oven which stood on stands at the side of two paraffin oil stoves, with the heat from these stoves going up into the oven. There was also a peat-fired range which had a rather unreliable oven, but Gwen used this too. Vacuuming was done with a sweeper and all washing was done by hand, using a washing board. Lighting came from oil lamps – tilly lamps - which had to be carefully maintained so that they worked efficiently. Even the streets in the village were lit with these lamps which hung from the walls and gave off a dim orange flicker. There was, however, the luxury of a battery-powered radio as batteries were readily available. Coal came to the island by puffer, but if there was stormy weather in the winter – a not infrequent occurrence – the puffer did not arrive and so there was no coal. Peat, therefore, was an important source of fuel and four lorry loads of peat were needed to keep the manse warm in the winter.

One of the deacons in the Bowmore church – Calum, a godly man whom Donald greatly admired – took Donald out to the peat banks and taught him how to cut peat. The process would start in March or April of each year. Calum would call for Donald early in the morning and they would walk out to the peat bank, accompanied by Calum's dog, Monty – named after Montgomery, the victor of Alamein. As they walked, Calum would talk to Donald in English and talk to the dog in Gaelic! Once at the peat bank, Calum would cut the peat slivers one by one and throw the wet cuts onto the grassy bank. Meanwhile, Donald was given a long pole with a fork at the end which he had to use to drive into the peat slivers, lift them and place them as far as his arms would allow him to carry them. This was to allow the peat to dry out. Calum had been cutting peat all his life and worked like a machine. Needless to say, Donald found it very hard to keep up with him, but he learned to do it and had the satisfaction of burning the peat in the winter months. In the middle of the peat cutting day, they would sit down and make some tea and Calum would say,

"Give thanks, Mr McCallum, give thanks. It is good to give thanks."

After the peat was cut there was more to be done before it could be taken home. Once one side of the peat was dry, it had to be turned and stacked so that the wind could blow through it and finish the drying process. Once dry, the peat had to be taken in a wheelbarrow to the roadside and built up into a big bing. A lorry was then hired to take the peat home and the final stage of the process was to wheelbarrow the peat into the peat shed at the manse.

"Peat warms you up three times over", remarked Donald, "one when you cut it, another when you bring it home and a third heat when you burn it!"

Donald had to pay the lorry driver eight shillings for every load of peat, so the four loads cost thirty two shillings. On top of this, he had to pay the Laird ten shillings a year for the privilege of cutting peat on his ground. Therefore, for forty two shillings – a little more than two pounds – he had his fuel for the winter, but it was a lot of very hard work.

The challenges faced by the very different living conditions were more than offset by the warmth of the people. After the anonymity of life in the city, merely walking down the street was an experience in itself. Anyone you met had to be greeted and engaged in conversation. Shopping was a lengthy process when you spoke to everyone you met on the way as well as the customers in each shop and, of course, the shopkeepers themselves. On one occasion, however, Gwen was away so long when doing shopping that Donald became quite worried. When she eventually returned, his first words were,

"What have you been doing all this time?"

He never forgot the story Gwen then told. She had been shopping for mince, taking with her the war-time ration coupons which were still needed, and had gone to one of the local butchers which was run by one of the women in the village. When Gwen asked for mince, the butcher said,

"I'll just get you some meat for the mince", and

disappeared into the back of the shop, returning with a whole carcass. Then she said to Gwen,

"The mincer's over there. You can get your mince."

Gwen began to mince the meat she needed, but before she was finished a number of other people came in for mince and Gwen had to continue mincing until they were all served. Every time she had minced just enough for one customer, another would come in and the butcher would look over at Gwen and say,

"There you are. She'll give you your mince!"

By the time she was finished, a couple of hours had gone past. From then on, Gwen would make rather more hasty visits to the butcher in case she was asked to mince the meat again! She did, however, continue to buy her mince from the butcher as it was the best mince she had ever tasted in her life!

Apart from coping with the everyday chores, when Donald and Gwen arrived in Islay they needed furniture. Strange though it may seem, they bought their first bed from the poorhouse in Bowmore. This was before the days of the National Health Service and the poorhouse was supported by the rates paid in Islay and Jura. With only four thousand people on Islay and two hundred people on Jura there must have been very little money available to support it. Islay had been an RAF base during the war and at that time the poorhouse had been stocked with bedding in case of air raids. Now the bedding was for sale, so they bought a couple of beds and some other items as well.

The manse garden was very big and needed a lot of cultivation. In this garden they were able to grow potatoes and other vegetables to supplement their diet and before long they also kept hens, thanks to one of Donald's uncles who had a smallholding near Campbeltown. Although rarely willing to leave Campbeltown, he came to Bowmore and after seeing that they had a lot of space in their garden sent them six hens – Black Leghorns. The hens arrived by post, in a large box. Donald looked inside the box and saw that they had laid some eggs on the journey. He therefore pushed up one of the spars on the box, just enough to lift out some eggs for tea, intending to let the hens out of their box after tea. However, when he came into the garden later, the hens were gone! A closer look showed that they had gathered in a nervous huddle at the bottom of the garden, but every time Donald approached them they fluttered away and eventually they all disappeared.

"Och!" thought Donald. "I've had the hens only an hour and I've lost them all already. How will I explain this to Uncle Jimmy?"

He thought he had better try to find them but the main problem was that so many other people in the neighbourhood kept hens and to Donald, at that time, one hen looked much the same as another. Gwen's sister, Margaret, was having a holiday with them at the time, so she accompanied Donald as he set off to find the hens. He told the old man in the next cottage about the hens and before long all the hens were back in the manse garden but instead of six he now had seven! One of Donald's neighbours was so sure the extra hen was Donald's that he had clipped its wings so it couldn't fly away again!

The Black Leghorns turned out to be marvellous layers, so Donald and Gwen acquired a Rhode Island Red, a quieter kind of bird for the purpose of sitting on eggs until they hatched. They also obtained a cockerel from one of the crofts and before long had a small poultry farm in their back garden. They put a dozen eggs under the Rhode Island Red and got six live chickens, but unfortunately five of the six were cockerels and they had wanted egg layers. As the cockerels grew they fought constantly and Donald had to separate them many times. Eventually they had the five males killed and used them as Christmas presents. At this time, just after the war, fresh chicken was very valuable and in short supply so the cockerels made very acceptable presents.

From time to time Gwen helped the District Nurse, covering for her when she went on holiday. Just before the nurse went on holiday one year, she told Gwen that there was one baby which might possibly arrive while Gwen was covering the district nurse's duties, but she fully expected to be back on Islay before the baby was born. A few days later, Donald and Gwen asked an elderly gentleman who lived on his own to come to the manse for tea. Gwen bought a chicken, a boiling fowl, and was just beginning to clean it when, at 7am, the doorbell rang. The baby was on its way and Gwen, in her capacity as district nurse, was needed immediately. She therefore had to leave the partially cleaned chicken, and go.

Donald fervently hoped that Gwen would return in time to finish cleaning the chicken, but time went by and still Gwen did not come home. He therefore had to finish cleaning and plucking the chicken before boiling it for the tea. When Gwen was finally free to return to the manse, she kept thinking all the way home,

"What will Donald have done with the chicken? He doesn't know how to prepare or cook it!"

However, as she climbed the stairs to the manse, her mind was put at rest as she could smell the chicken and realised that Donald had managed to put it on to cook. She opened the door to see Donald and the old gentleman sitting comfortably while the boiling pot bubbled away nicely. Gwen thought Donald had done a wonderful job, but teased him afterwards by saying that she had ignored the feathers floating on top of the water as the chicken boiled!

Meanwhile, Donald had to settle down to the work of a pastor and also study for exams. The Baptist Union had stated that if Donald went to Bowmore he would be expected to work for and pass the Baptist Union exams. He had not studied since leaving school at the age of fifteen, so it was very hard to acquire the habit of regular reading. There were plenty of things to keep Donald occupied around the manse and the garden, apart from the pastoral work, but Gwen was very firm with him, making sure that he studied regularly. Although the manse had a little study with built-in book shelves, Donald had very few books and so had to acquire the books he needed for his exams. However, once settled into the routine of study he definitely enjoyed it. The first really theological book he read was part of some studies on the Old Testament. As he began to read he thought,

"How will I ever absorb this stuff? Why doesn't the author write in clear English so that I can understand it?"

He read the book straight through to get the feel of it and then afterwards re-read the book bit by bit, in a more detailed way. It was not long before he found that this was a good way to study and made this method his habit when beginning a new book. The exams frightened him a bit, but he managed to cope, passing all of them at the first attempt. Several weeks after sitting the exams, the results arrived through the post. On each occasion, Donald was reluctant to open the letter, afraid of what it might contain. When he opened the envelope and found he had passed he could not believe it and announced to Gwen,

"The day of miracles has not passed!"

From time to time, ministers would come to the island on holiday and sometimes take a church service. One of these ministers gave Donald some advice which he admitted he all too readily followed:

"Avoid housework like the plague!"

Gwen was rather annoyed at the advice and at Donald's ready acceptance of it, but both realised what the minister actually meant: he was pointing out to Donald the need for self discipline in his role as a minister. In those days, just the business of living in the island, with all the work in the house and garden, took up a lot of time, so Donald was being reminded that the minister needs to keep his eyes on the work God has given him to do – preach and minister to his flock - and should therefore not allow himself to be too distracted by the needs of the house and garden. He had to be able to work at home, preparing for Sunday services; also, there was the need to visit the congregation and be ready to be called on at all times of the day or night. It soon became clear that this was a way of life, rather than a job, and both Donald and Gwen were more than willing to live such a lifestyle.

One of Donald's duties was to be chaplain to the

Poorhouse in Bowmore. His concern for the poor and the marginalised in society persisted throughout his ministry and he often showed his concern for the people to whom he ministered in the Poorhouse. These were the days before the National Health Service when there was very little money available to care for those who lived in places like the Poorhouse, so conditions were rather sparse. Donald spoke up for the residents on a number of occasions, one time being told he was 'an interfering young man' when he asked for something for an old man who was very ill. Fortunately, the National Health Service brought money to improve conditions and Donald was glad to see this happen.

On his first visit to Islay, when he was being considered for the post of Baptist Minister, he was asked to take a service in the Poorhouse. It was then that he realised he had no idea how to conduct a service for them! He was more used to speaking to young men but he thought quickly and decided that they would certainly know a psalm, so he asked,

"Would you like to sing a psalm, Psalm 23?"

The words were barely out of his mouth when an old man rose up out of his chair and went out of the room, saying that he would go and fetch Sam. It turned out that Sam was a young man who lived in the Poorhouse and worked in the gardens there. Once Sam arrived, the service continued and Donald felt very much at home ministering to these people.

When Donald and Gwen went to Islay, the membership of the Bowmore congregation was twenty-six, but they were scattered all over the island and could not easily come to church on a Sunday. Quite a few of them lived out in the country on crofts and one of Donald's duties was to go every two weeks and take a service for them in one of the crofts. The crofters gave Donald and Gwen a lovely welcome, making them feel very much at home. Sometimes hens would run in and out as the service took place and then after the service there would be delicious homemade oatcakes to eat.

After a while, Donald thought that there were a lot of folk in these areas who would like to come to the service in the croft but would find it difficult to make their way to someone else's house. He therefore managed to get the use of an old RAF hut at Balinaby which had been used in the war but was no longer in use. He then asked the church to hire a car so that he could go there on a Sunday afternoon. Later, as numbers at the service grew, he hired a larger vehicle to go round the island picking people up and bringing them to the service. Eventually, he had quite a big service in the RAF hut every second Sunday. There was also another place where he would lead a Sunday afternoon service once a month, so on three Sundays each month he would be out in the country leading an afternoon service. While he was out preaching in the country on a Sunday afternoon, Gwen would help another lady, Freda, take the Sunday school. She also often played the piano or the organ for church services.

Many a Sunday Donald conducted four services: the service in the Poor House where he was chaplain, the morning service in Bowmore Baptist church, the service in the RAF hut and then the evening service in the Bowmore church, followed by the youth fellowship. This was a punishing schedule, but he was young and fit and well able to cope with the demands of such a busy day. At first, however, he found it difficult to preach a long enough sermon. On one occasion, when the service in Bowmore lasted less than an hour a visitor to the church complained about the brevity of the sermon!

However, help was at hand. Each time Gwen's father came to Islay he preached in the Baptist church and spent time helping Donald to construct his sermons. Gwen's father had been preaching for many years and was well known as a good preacher, so his help was invaluable. Donald readily took his advice and it was not long before Donald felt more confident in both the preparation and the preaching of sermons. A cursory glance at Donald's sermons and those of his father-in-law clearly shows the similarity in structure, a lesson obviously well learned, for in later years Donald became a well-known preacher in his own right.

Both Donald and Gwen threw themselves into the work on Islay and it was not long before the church began to grow. The first service of Believers' Baptism for sixteen years in the Baptist Church in Bowmore was an exciting event for all involved. There was much to be done to prepare for the baptismal service, including the filling of the baptismal tank with water. There were no taps to fill the tank, so a metal chute from the manse to the church was constructed and fed through a window in the church into the baptistry. In order to ensure that the water was warm enough, Donald and Gwen ran up and down the stairs connecting the church and the manse, carrying boiling water. All their preparations meant that the baptismal tank was warm enough and the whole service went very well.

The interior of Bowmore Baptist Church in the late 1940s

In addition to the Sunday services, there was a weekly prayer meeting, often held in the home of an older person who was unable to attend church regularly. This allowed the older folk to feel part of the church family and proved to be a blessing to many.

During the week, Donald often spent the morning working in his study before going out visiting in the afternoons. If his visits involved going a long way into the country, he would have to leave in the morning, for all his visits were made on his bicycle and it could take a whole day to cycle up into the country, visit the families and cycle back home again. He continued these visits by bicycle into the winter months when the days were shorter, meaning that he had to come home in the dark. This could be a problem at times as the roads were not well made and there was no electricity on the island until 1948.

In his visiting, Donald went to crofts which were rather isolated. His visit was quite an occasion and he was given a great welcome. At one of the crofts, Kindrochaidh, there was always a ritual when he visited. The woman on the croft hard boiled two eggs, then brought out a great lump of cheese and finally put home made bannocks on the table. She would sit at one side of the table and Donald would sit at the other and then she would say,

"Now Mr McCallum, take your tea."

Donald was very glad of the food, for it was a long cycle back to Bowmore, especially if there was a strong wind.

Donald was not simply concerned for the Baptists on Islay. Indeed, from the beginning of his time on the island, Donald had consistently good relationships with the parish ministers and occasionally preached in the Round Church in Bowmore. On their first Christmas in Islay, Neil Ross, the parish minister at the time, invited Donald and Gwen for a meal in the huge Church of Scotland manse. By then Neil Ross was a very old man who had stayed on in the ministry beyond retirement age because the young men were not available during the war years. A Gaelic scholar, he was able to preach in both Gaelic and English. By 1946, however, he was so frail that his congregation worried that he might fall as he went up into the pulpit on a Sunday. The result of this was that when there was any church work to be done, Donald and Gwen did it - and they were glad to do it.

It was Neil Ross' frailty that led to Donald becoming involved with some of the schools on the island: as he was too frail to be a chaplain to the schools, Donald was asked to take his place and visit the high school in the village and the primary schools in the surrounding countryside at least once a month. The education authority paid for a car to take him around all the schools he had to visit. Donald enjoyed this aspect of his ministry and soon got to know the young people very well.

He enjoyed being with the young folk. Alan Bell – one of the young boys in the village at that time – remembers an incident during the severe winter of 1947 when there was snow lying in the village.

"We boys were ranged on one side of the main street while Mr McCallum was walking down the other side. He spied us, picked up snowballs, and immediately battle commenced. This was our new Baptist minister!"

Another memory is when Donald joined in games of football with the boys.

"As was our wont, several of us were kicking a ball about the football pitch when Mr McCallum appeared and joined in our game. He was not a great footballer – more dash than control – but he obviously enjoyed running about with the boys."

When a new young minister came to the parish church, he and Donald worked together to provide for the young people of Bowmore. One of the young people at that time, Robert Forrest, commented on Donald and Gwen's ministry in the following way:

"What an impact their ministry had on the island, and especially on those of us fortunate enough to be counted among the youth of that post-war era. Mr McCallum set up a Boy Scouts troop in Bowmore, and underpinning all of the usual Scouting activities [First aid; tying knots; camping, football etc.] was his strong Christian ethic, which transformed itself to all of us who came under his sphere of influence.

Rev McCallum's ministry in the Baptist Church coincided with that of the Rev Murdo MacRae in the Round Kirk and they were a splendid team together. They formed the Bowmore Boys Club and inculcated Christian values to all our sporting activities, and drew from their respective strengths – the 'Celtic fire' of Murdo MacRae and the gentle evangelism of Donald McCallum. The greatest thing about Donald, as far as I am concerned, was that whether he preached with his mouth or not, he declared by the light in his eye and the decision of his bearing that he was a man saturated in Christ."

The cooperation between Donald and his fellow minister, Murdo MacRae, was not confined to youth work. Together they organised an open air service on summer evenings at the pier in Bowmore. Unfortunately the midges became too much to cope with and the congregation had to retreat!

While Donald was organising Scouts and the Boys Club, playing football and cycling with the boys, Gwen became friendly with the girls and organised a handicrafts class where she taught them leather work. She sent to the mainland for the leather and asked the girls up to the manse to try their hand at making purses. This was a successful venture and soon both Donald and Gwen knew the young people in the village very well, quickly forming good relationships with them. They were both young, with lots of energy, and with no family of their own at that time they were able to spend a lot of time with the young people.

Donald took the boys on holiday to Canty Bay, the property owned by the Charlotte Chapel Scouts. Situated on the coast of East Lothian, just opposite the Bass

Rock, it was a wonderful place for a camp and the boys thoroughly enjoyed themselves. There was, however, one scary moment just after they all arrived in Edinburgh on their way to Canty Bay when one boy was so fascinated with Princes Street that he did not realise that he should look out for traffic and was almost knocked over as they crossed the road. Donald just managed to get him out of the way in time. On a happier note, an outing to the zoo was made particularly memorable when the boys threw chewing gum to the monkeys!

While the boys were enjoying Canty Bay, Gwen took the girls to the Christian Endeavour Home at Tighnabruaich. Many of the girls had hardly been out of their own village before because of the lack of public transport on Islay, so they loved the adventure of a holiday away from the island.

Back on Islay, Donald and Gwen got to know the older folk too. Donald was particularly impressed with the deacons in the church who were such good men and so dependable. He felt that he learned so much from them during these early years of ministry and he never forgot their encouragement when he was a raw recruit with so much to learn. These men and the older women in the congregation gave him so much help and encouragement that it had a profound effect on his pastoring and preaching ministries and for the rest of his life he felt that he owed them a tremendous debt of thanks. These people were all ordinary working folk, but in their Christian lives they were near to the heart of God. Many years later – just before his retirement – Donald was asked to speak on Scottish Television's programme 'Late Call' and he used the opportunity to express this debt of gratitude, naming the deacons who had given him such help at the start of his ministry.

Calum, who taught Donald to cut peat, was very deaf and quite unable to hear what was being said in a church service. In spite of this, he regularly came to church where he somehow sensed the atmosphere and would tell Donald when he thought it had been a good service. He used to sit at the back and give out the books as the people came in. However, this changed when he acquired a hearing aid as he then sat at the front of the church. The hearing aid, for which he had to save up, was a big box which was hanging over his chest, suspended from his neck. Once the ear piece was in place, Calum would tune in the box until he got on to the correct wavelength and as he did this there would be a wailing noise until he was on the right frequency. Once settled, he would fold his arms, sit back and listen to the sermon, drinking everything in. For the first time for many years he was able to participate fully in a service and it meant so much to him.

Calum was one person whom Donald could never forget, because he taught him so much about life's real qualities. Along with the other older men and women in the church, he taught Donald how to live a Christian life in a community where life was lived in front of everyone else because the community was so small. These people were respected because of the quality of their lives and both Donald and Gwen held them in high regard.

Although Donald and Gwen loved Islay, there were some difficult times as well as happy ones. One difficult experience came when they looked after a dog for a short while. One day, Gwen came out of the house with the dog and was crossing the road when a cow appeared from behind a shed with a little calf behind her. As soon as the cow saw the dog, she went for it and then turned her attention to Gwen. Before Gwen realised what was happening, she was up on the horns of the cow and was tossed over a wall. Gwen was knocked out, but the dog chased the cow away. When she came round, the dog was licking her face. As a result of this incident, Gwen had a lump on her head and was badly shaken. However, neither Donald nor Gwen wanted to make any fuss as they knew the owner of the cow and also realised how much they themselves had to learn about life in the countryside. When the folk in the village found out about the incident they said that Donald and Gwen should have told them. Although it was commonplace to see cattle in the streets of the village, the cow had just calved and should not have been out on the road. Needless to say, Gwen has been wary of cows ever since!

There were sad times too. Gwen had two miscarriages, losing both babies when the pregnancies were well into the fourth month. This was very hard for her, especially when she was so far from her own family. After one of the miscarriages, a friend from Gwen's nursing days came for a holiday and found Gwen ill in bed. Instead of relaxing on holiday, she then spent her time looking after Gwen.

There was a family tragedy with the death of Donald's sister, Margaret, who died of cancer. Donald, knowing how ill she was, left Islay in a hurry to go home to be with her and arrived just before she died. Donald remarked,

"I saw a lot of death in the war, but it's different when it's your own kin."

After Margaret's death Donald's mother, who had

stayed on in Edinburgh with Donald's sisters, came to stay in Bowmore. Gwen greatly admired her because of her strong faith and the way she coped with increasing ill-health. Without any fuss, she quickly adapted to the very different lifestyle on the island.

As time went on, Donald and Gwen continued to love Islay, growing close to the island community. However, in the summer of 1949 a couple from Pilton in Edinburgh came to the island on holiday. As a result of their visit to the church in Bowmore, they spoke to their son-in-law who was the church secretary of Granton Baptist Church in Edinburgh, saying,

"You should see if you can persuade the minister in Bowmore to come to Granton."

When the Granton church did call him, Donald felt it was the right move to make and in January 1950 Donald and Gwen moved to Edinburgh to begin a very different type of ministry. The removal to Granton cost £60 for one covered van load and this included packing. Donald and Gwen knew they would miss the island people whom they had come to love, but looked forward to the challenge of ministry in an Edinburgh housing scheme. Gwen was once again expecting a baby and this time, they hoped and prayed, there would not be a miscarriage.

The people of Islay were sorry to say goodbye to Donald and Gwen, but many kept in touch over the following months and years. Alan Bell – one of the young people in Bowmore at the time – later paid tribute to their ministry in the following way:

"It is difficult to summarise the contribution Mr McCallum made to the people of Islay, and Bowmore in

particular. His natural exuberance, youthful outlook and empathy with youngsters, allied to the goodness and godliness of the man, allowed him to identify with all members of the island community – no matter their status or denomination. The support given by his wife Gwen cannot be underestimated, for she shared in a ministry that has left an indelible mark on all those who came into contact with this remarkable Christian."

Chapter 7

Edinburgh – a new housing area

After the years in Islay, at first it seemed strange to be back in a city, but Donald and Gwen soon settled into their new life. They had both been brought up in a city, so adjusted quickly to the change from country life. The next six years would bring many more changes and challenges.

Granton Baptist Church had been founded in 1940 by the Edinburgh Baptist Association and was in the middle of the new housing scheme of Pilton in Edinburgh. When Donald and Gwen arrived there, the area was still growing and had a population of about thirty thousand. After three years on Islay which had a population of only about four thousand, this was a very different kind of life. Started in 1938, the Pilton development was ideal for young families moving into these newer homes after the war and then settling down to bring up their families.

When Donald and Gwen first arrived in January 1950, the membership of the church was sixty five and Sunday services were held in a hut which had belonged to the Buttercup Dairy Farm. Although probably originally intended for hens, the hut had never been used for its original purpose, instead becoming a place of worship for a new, and growing, congregation. In January 1950 the hut was too small to accommodate all those who wanted to come to the welcome service for the new young minister and his wife, so the celebrations were held in a local school. During the course of the evening, one of the ladies presented Gwen with a bouquet of flowers, assuring her that the women in the church were very friendly and adding,

"In this church if you want things done, you'll find the women are the boys!"

Donald and Gwen never forgot these words. Indeed, they soon found out that the women played a big part in church life and it was not long before Gwen made many friends and became very involved in running the large women's meeting.

From the beginning, the work in Granton just grew and it was quite obvious that the hen hut was too small for the growing congregation. On a good summer's day there could be so many people attending the Sunday services that the side door of the hut had to be opened. This caused a draught which kept blowing Donald's sermon notes off their stand! On the other hand, if the door had to be opened in the winter, the congregation froze. The hut had served its purpose and it was time for a new building.

Well before Donald's arrival in Granton, the congregation had realised their need for a larger building and had begun a building fund. At Donald's first business meeting, in May 1950, a Building Fund Committee was set up and work towards the new building began in earnest.

However, soon after the business meeting Donald began to feel very unwell. Since returning to Edinburgh Gwen had noticed that he often complained about being cold. She could not understand this as he had been brought up in Edinburgh and so was well used to the cold winds which the city can experience. Now, in late May 1950, he had been in Edinburgh only a few months but was feeling constantly exhausted. One morning he set off from home to conduct a local school assembly. These assemblies were a regular event, but on this occasion after walking the short distance to the school he felt so drained that he had to sit down to conduct the assembly. Only a few months before this, he had been fit enough to cycle all over Islay. Before long he also began to be extremely thirsty.

"I could have drunk the ocean dry and never quenched my thirst," he remarked.

He just could not understand what was happening to him.

Gwen, however, with her nurse's training had a good idea what was wrong and called the doctor who immediately took a urine sample from Donald, telling Gwen to phone later that day for the result. As the doctor went out of the door he said,

"I hope it's not what I think it is, but phone me tonight."

Donald had a deacons' meeting that evening and there was no phone in the manse at that time, so Gwen went to the nearest phone box and dialled the doctor's number. The test results confirmed Gwen's fears – Donald had been diagnosed diabetic. It soon became clear that he had Type 1 diabetes which would mean insulin injections for the rest of his life. Gwen was advised to watch his diet carefully until he could be admitted to hospital.

The diagnosis was a big blow. As soon as he was in hospital, Donald was on insulin injections, two a day. He also had to learn how to cope with a very restricted diet and a limited intake of food, weighing everything he ate to make sure that he consumed the correct quantities to cope with the amount of insulin he was told to take. It was a balancing act and in 1950 was a huge challenge because so little was known about the treatment of diabetics. In the first few months after the diagnosis he found it very hard to adjust to such a restricted diet, often feeling so hungry that he had to be given pills to suppress his appetite. At that time the diabetic's diet and insulin regime were very strict, with little flexibility to suit individual needs. Worst of all for Donald was the fact that he was not allowed to eat bananas – his favourite food! Fortunately, the diet became much less restricted in later years and bananas were once more on the menu.

There was another change in store while Donald was in hospital, but this time a much happier one. Gwen's pregnancy had progressed satisfactorily and by the time Donald was admitted to hospital the baby was due in just over one month. One morning Donald had a surprise when his mother arrived in the ward, saying,

"Gwen's in the maternity ward downstairs."

This was the beginning of June and the baby was not due until the beginning of July, so Donald was a little anxious. He went down to Gwen's ward and was able to see her before he was chased away by the nursing staff.

"Husbands in those days were thought to be quite surplus to requirements when it came to babies being born!" he later remarked.

By the end of the day Donald was proudly looking at his newborn daughter, Ruth Miriam - one month premature and weighing only five and a half pounds, but healthy. He often reminisced about that moment:

"I never forgot what she looked like. I held her in my hands. She was perfectly formed, even down to her fingernails and I thought, 'This is a miracle.'"

As soon as he was given permission, he took his new daughter upstairs to the men's ward to show her off to the nurses and his fellow patients.

It was not long before Donald, Gwen and Ruth were all home. However, the month of June had one more family event, unfortunately a sad one: Gwen's father died suddenly. He had continued to preach almost every Sunday, doing most of his travelling to churches by bicycle. Although he had not felt too well on a number of occasions, he continued his very active lifestyle. One Sunday in the middle of June he preached in a church in Wales and stayed overnight in a hotel, intending to cycle home in the morning. However, he was found dead in his hotel room, having taken ill and died in his sleep during the night. This was a very sad time and Gwen, with a newborn, premature baby, was unable to go to Birmingham for the funeral.

In the five months since leaving Bowmore Donald's and Gwen's lives had gone through enormous changes. The delight at the safe arrival of their daughter was immense. After the heartbreaking experience of two miscarriages, the birth of Ruth made such a wonderful difference to them both. On the other hand, coping with diabetes was a huge challenge as Donald had never known illness in his life. Working in a growing church which demanded so much time and energy it was an awful feeling to have such a diagnosis, but the church members were very supportive. Gwen's nursing training was put to good use and with her constant help and support Donald soon learned to cope. On top of all this, Gwen had to adjust to the loss of her father.

However, in the midst of all these personal changes the Granton church continued to grow. Donald was always grateful for the dedication shown by the deacons in Granton, many of whom had left behind large prosperous churches in order to support an extension church in a housing scheme. They willingly gave of their time and energy for the sake of God's kingdom.

The proposed new church building soon occupied a lot of Donald's time and attention. Donald hoped to persuade the Baptist Union of Scotland to give some financial help. He felt he was being rather cheeky to ask for such help, but nevertheless he invited the Union's Secretary, Treasurer and President to come to Granton to look at the situation and consider whether any help was possible.

"The night they came was a wet one," Donald remarked, "and so it was rather ideal for the purpose at hand. They all sat in the hut as the rain poured down."

The Baptist Union office-bearers knew the congregation was growing and had every expectation that it would continue to grow. They asked a few questions and then said, to the delight of those gathered to meet them,

"If we loan you some money, do you think you could find one thousand pounds?"

The cost of the new building was to be in the region

of £10,000. Church members would be expected to raise £1000 by the time the building was completed, the Baptist Union would loan £1000 which had to be repaid within ten years and they would also contribute another £3000 towards the total. In addition, there would be more than £5000 available from the sale of Marshall Street Baptist Church in Edinburgh's city centre, which had closed down in 1943. The congregation of that church, before they dispersed, had willed the money from the sale of their building to a new Baptist extension cause in Edinburgh – a wonderful inheritance for the Granton folk.

"That was listening to God," said Donald. "They knew that Granton would need a new building, even although in 1943 it was still in a temporary trial period and, in human terms, not necessarily going to be permanent."

By May 1951, various estimates for the building had been received by the church and tenders had been accepted. As the building progressed, Donald became more and more involved, becoming an unofficial 'clerk of works' as he made daily checks on progress. The congregation gave sacrificially, raising the required money, even when costs escalated and the final total was £12,000 rather than the original estimate of £10,000. Typical of many, one of the older women in the congregation even saved up pennies and halfpennies in a jar.

The new building, with seating for about 250 people, was formally opened on Saturday 20th December 1952. It was a very exciting time for the church and sparked off a new period of growth. Church members took great pride in their new building and made sure that it was kept clean and tidy. The building was not without its difficulties, though. The heating system never worked properly. The MacMillan hot air system, supposed to bring hot air from the boiler into the church, was never adequate and was soon affectionately renamed the 'McCallum' hot air system! It was many years before the source of the problem with the heating was discovered.

Billy Graham was in Scotland in the spring of 1954 and he made the Christian faith a talking point, so Donald came up with the idea of having a series of Sunday evening sermons on matters which concerned people. He asked members of the church to provide him with the questions that bothered them, questions which they themselves could not answer. He also made his own list of questions and talked them all over with a young American man who was attending services at Granton and who often enjoyed speaking to Donald about what was going on in the church. Between them, they came up with a list of questions which formed the basis of a series of sermons entitled 'Your question and the Christian answer'.

Donald told the church members what he intended to do and said,

"Here's the bargain! I will do the preaching, we'll all do the praying, but you need to contact friends and neighbours to provide the congregation."

The bargain was kept! Church members delivered leaflets about the special services and encouraged their friends to come, with the result that the new church filled up and was packed to the door. At the first service, one of the church girls walked in with two other girls Donald had never seen before. They had to take the front seats because there were no other seats left.

At each service, Donald preached about a different question: 'Is there a God?' 'Is the Bible true?' 'Why is there so much suffering in the world?' 'Does God answer our prayers?' 'What happens when we die?' 'How do Christians enjoy themselves?' The last sermon in the series was entitled, 'Make up your mind!' At the end of that service, sixteen people responded and came to faith in Christ that night.

This started off a period of conversions. Donald was excited each time he preached because he realised that God was at work among the people who came to the services, but he never knew exactly what might happen.

"People were just getting converted right, left and centre. And that was the truth," Donald remarked.

A typical story was that of a young couple, Jim and Molly Fleming, who were considering sending their daughter to a Sunday School somewhere, although they themselves were not attending church. A friend who lived close to Granton Baptist suggested that they might like to send their daughter to the Sunday School there, but also invited them to go to a church service and hear the minister preach about questions which people were asking.

One night, they decided to hear for themselves what the minister was saying. As they listened, they realised that they were hearing answers to questions they had been thinking about, so as they left the church after the service they spoke to Donald at the door and asked if he would come to their home and talk with them. He went to see them that very night and found that they had only one question to ask him,

"How do we become Christians?"

Once Donald explained, they knelt at the sofa in their sitting room and committed their lives to Christ. They had found what they were seeking in life.

They began to attend church regularly, feeling very much at home among the people there, and within a few weeks were baptised as believers. It was not long before they wanted to tell others of their new-found faith. They did not live in Pilton but in another big housing area nearby, Drylaw, where there was no Sunday school, so they started a Sunday school in their street. There was not enough room for all the children in their house, so the Sunday school took place in the street! The flats had balconies and neighbours would lean over their balconies to hear what was going on. After working within Granton Baptist Church for some time, they moved away to full-time Christian service with the Fisherman's Mission in Scotland and then went as missionaries to Zimbabwe.

The story of Jim and Molly Fleming's conversion was typical of the exciting ways in which God was growing His church in Granton at that time. Many people were converted and there was a period of great blessing. Church members were constantly bringing new people to services as well as taking part in church activities with great enthusiasm. Services of Believers' Baptism were exciting times, with sometimes ten or more people being baptised at the one service. Donald and Gwen were fully involved in the life of the church and Donald faithfully preached God's Word Sunday by Sunday. Donald's mother, who continued to live with them, also took part in church activities, as much as her health would allow. The church was recording substantial growth, such as the thirty-seven new members added to the membership roll in the eighteen months between November 1953 and May 1955.

One young person who came to the church at this time was a girl named Eleanor, from the island of Colonsay. She came to Edinburgh to do a course at college and, as she had attended the Baptist Church in Colonsay, looked for a similar church she could attend in Edinburgh. Before long, she found Granton Baptist Church and began to come to services there. When she returned home to Colonsay at the end of her course, the church there no longer had a minister, so she asked Donald if he would send her some of his sermon notes so that she could read them to the congregation. Donald was happy to do this and sent sermon notes to her for many years. Eleanor kept in touch and Donald went to Colonsay to perform the wedding ceremony when Eleanor was married and, on another occasion, to be present at the baptism of Eleanor's husband, Alasdair. There was no baptistry in the Colonsay church, so the baptism took place in the sea.

While the Granton church was growing, Donald was becoming more used to life as a diabetic. Gwen kept a close eye on him, but there were some difficult times when his diabetes caused problems. He was very sensitive to insulin and could quickly become 'hypo', needing extra sugar very speedily to cope with the insulin he had to take. However, in spite of the problems he coped extremely well and gradually the diet became a little more palatable. One story, however, makes clear the lack of knowledge about diabetes in the early 1950s.

At the beginning of his time in Granton, Donald had to study for his final Baptist Union exams. Much to his surprise, he soon passed them all and was fully registered with the Baptist Union of Scotland as a minister. He then decided that it would be sensible to be registered with the equivalent Union in England, just in case God ever called him to a church there. He therefore wrote to the Secretary of the Baptist Union of Great Britain and Ireland, asking if he could be registered with them, but was turned down, simply because he was diabetic. When Donald wrote again, the reply was still the same.

A fellow minister in Edinburgh was so incensed about the treatment of Donald's application that he wrote a letter on Donald's behalf. The result was yet another letter to Donald, this time stating that if his health improved in the years to come, they might reconsider their decision. Donald replied, saying that diabetes was a life-long condition, and then gave up trying to be registered with the Baptist Union of Great Britain and Ireland. His friend, however, had the last word: he again wrote back on Donald's behalf, this time stating that even St Paul would not have been accepted for registration under their terms! His friend's remarks must have had some effect for in 1956 Donald finally achieved the registration he had sought.

Gwen had her own difficulties too. She and Donald had both grown up as part of a family with brothers and sisters and were keen that Ruth should not be an only child. Unfortunately, by 1953 Gwen had had two more miscarriages, again losing the babies when well into the fourth month of the pregnancy. Doctors could find no apparent reason for the miscarriages, but they continued to happen. This was heartbreaking.

It was at this point that Donald and Gwen decided to

adopt a child. They approached the Church of Scotland Adoption Society and were accepted as adoptive parents. It was therefore with great delight that on 1st February 1954, Donald's birthday, they went to a nursery to collect their new son, whom they named Donald Peter, although he was to be known as Peter. They took Ruth with them, going by train to the town where the baby was being looked after in a nursery. When they arrived home, Donald's mother and aunt, along with two members of the Granton church, were waiting for them. "They've got big hearts," commented Donald's mother as she was introduced to her grandson for the first time.

Peter, at six weeks old, was a small baby, but he thrived under Gwen's expert care and was soon the pride of the local baby clinic! The church folk were also delighted and fully supported Donald and Gwen in the adoption.

As the church continued to grow, members of other Baptist churches in Scotland began to hear about Granton Baptist Church and its young minister. In 1955, the minister of Stirling Baptist Church, John Rigley, retired after a long and godly ministry through the years of war and the first ten years after the war. The deacons of the church were looking for someone who would build on the good work done by John Rigley and would also have a powerful spiritual impact both in the church and in the community, particularly in relation to young people. Therefore, having heard of the tremendous growth of the Granton church and the way it was reaching out to the community around it, they asked Donald if he would allow himself to be considered for the position of minister in Stirling.

Donald and Gwen on a bus trip with the Granton church in the early 1950s

At first Donald was very reluctant to move from Granton, where he and his family were so happy and where God was doing new things constantly. However, the Stirling deacons persisted in their request and, after much agonising over the decision, Donald accepted the call to Stirling Baptist Church. For the rest of his life he said this decision was the hardest he ever had to make.

At the end of June 1956, Donald and Gwen said farewell to their many friends in Granton and prepared for the move to Stirling. After a family holiday on the island of Colonsay, they moved into the manse in Stirling and a service of induction took place, attended by a good number of Granton folks. Donald had always appreciated the choir in Granton, often telling them how good they were and how much he enjoyed their singing. However, when the Granton choir heard the beautiful singing of the Stirling choir at the induction, one of the girls said to Donald,

"After hearing that, you can't still say we are the best choir in Scotland."

Donald's reply was typical of his humour:

"No," he said, "but you're still the best looking!"

The years in Granton had seen great blessing, with Church membership growing from 65 to 167 in six action-packed years. There had also been life-changing circumstances for both Donald and Gwen. They were very sad to leave Granton, but looked forward expectantly to new and exciting days ahead during the years in Stirling.

Chapter 8

Stirling – a market town

The move to Stirling brought many changes for the whole family, with the first obvious change being the size of the manse. In Edinburgh, Donald and Gwen had lived in an upper cottage flat in the Pilton area, where their bedroom doubled as Donald's study. The manse in Stirling, however, was a large semi-detached Victorian house, situated in Albert Place in the King's Park area, a very desirable part of the town. The house was built over three floors and had a total of eleven rooms – nine good sized rooms and two box-rooms. Donald loved the spaciousness of the house and enjoyed the beautiful view from his study on the top floor; however, keeping such a large house clean and tidy was a lot of work for Gwen. Furnishing a house of this size was also a challenge, but gradually more furniture was acquired and the house began to fill up. In the first few years a stair carpet for the long flight of stone stairs to the first floor was just too expensive, so Donald and Gwen bought rubber mats and glued them onto the stairs. Later, a generous gift allowed a stair carpet to be purchased.

Such a large house was also difficult to heat. Donald's

mother, who was often ill, needed to be kept warm, and since becoming diabetic Donald had found cold weather difficult to cope with. He was therefore very glad when the church had a Rayburn stove put into the kitchen. This made a huge difference to the temperature in the house and, in the absence of central heating, provided much needed warmth as well as a constant source of hot water. On a cold winter's day, the warmest person in the house was the one nearest to the Rayburn! Gwen used the oven in the Rayburn to produce wonderful baking, very much appreciated by the many visitors who enjoyed manse hospitality over the years.

The manse garden was large, so Donald was able to indulge his passion for growing potatoes, along with a wide variety of fruits and vegetables. He particularly liked the fruit trees which had been planted when the house was built but which were still producing juicy apples and plums almost one hundred years later. The plums were so abundant that Donald boasted,

"You only need to stand under a tree, open your mouth and a plum drops in!"

Gwen made jam from the various garden fruits, while Ruth and Peter happily invited friends along to help them pick – and eat – the abundant harvest of plums.

Gwen, a keen gardener, enjoyed cultivating flowers. In the summer, she often managed to find some time to have morning coffee or afternoon tea out in the garden so that she could enjoy the sun. On a cold, but sunny, spring or autumn day she would even wrap up in a warm coat and sit on the bench in the back garden to have her morning coffee. Donald claimed she was a sun worshipper!

Work in the church began almost as soon as Donald arrived in Stirling. The act of induction to Stirling Baptist Church took place during the morning service on Sunday 29th July 1956. The whole family attended the induction – Donald, Gwen, Ruth and Peter, along with Donald's mother, his sister Ruby and brother-in-law Willie Dudgeon. In the evening, once again the family set off for the church service, this time leaving Willie to look after Peter who was too young to attend, being only two and a half. During the course of the evening, Willie realised that Peter had disappeared. He could not find him anywhere and was beginning to be very worried when Peter suddenly appeared in front of him shouting,

"I's hiding!"

Peter had had a wonderful time hiding in the large house, completely unaware of the worry he had caused. He had hidden in a small cloakroom beside the front door, a room which could easily be overlooked when hunting for a small boy.

A large number of people from Granton attended the induction social on the Monday evening. This took place in the South Parish Church, across the road from the Baptist Church, with approximately 500 attending. It was hard to say goodbye once again to the Granton folk, but the large numbers of Stirling people attending the social indicated that they were looking forward with great anticipation to the ministry which was now beginning.

One of Donald's first experiences, however, had a link to the past. Shortly after arriving in Stirling, Donald received a card from the hospital. In those days, cards were sent to inform ministers in the town when any members of the church were in hospital and therefore unable to attend church on a Sunday. Donald looked at the name on the card – a Mrs Cowan – but did not recognise the name. He then looked at the church membership roll to see if her name was there. To his surprise, there was no Mrs Cowan and he certainly could not remember ever having met anyone of that name. However, he went up to the hospital to see the lady. It turned out that she had known Donald's father when he was stationed in Stirling Castle. While in Stirling, he had regularly met with a group of Christians in King Street and Mrs Cowan had been one of his fellow worshippers. On reading in the Stirling Observer of a Donald McCallum being inducted to the Baptist Church she had wondered if he was related to the Duncan McCallum she had known so many years earlier. She had therefore registered as a Baptist with the hospital so that she could find out! Mrs Cowan's daughter later became a member of Stirling Baptist Church.

Donald also visited church members and friends in their homes. One person he regularly visited was a Mrs Richardson who lived on her own in the town centre and was in her nineties. Concerned about her, he went to check on her every night to make sure that she was safe. She loved to come out to church and, once Donald had a car, he would quite often bring her to church. One wet, miserable evening as she was holding onto his arm on the way to the car she remarked,

"A'm I no daft comin' oot on a nicht like this!"

She became quite excited at the idea of reaching her hundredth birthday and after her ninety-eighth birthday remarked to Donald,

"Twa years fae noo we'll hae some fun!"

Regrettably, her wish was not fulfilled for she did not live to be one hundred.

The congregation in Stirling was widely scattered throughout the town and in the surrounding farms and villages. At first, Donald cycled or took a bus when visiting church people, but this meant that a single visit could take up a lot of his time. The offer of a car for only £5 was too good to miss, so Donald became the proud owner of an old Austin 7 Ruby Saloon with wire wheels and a sliding fabric sun roof. He bought the car from a lady in Stirling Baptist Church who also taught him the basic driving skills. It was the time of the Suez crisis when learner drivers were allowed to drive unaccompanied, so once Donald had mastered the basics he had several months driving on his own before his driving test. He passed the test first time. Donald was convinced that the tester had seen enough of the old car and did not want to risk going in it again!

Donald's first car

It was not long before he was doing a huge mileage, visiting people in villages as far apart as Braco, Milnathort and Balfron. The car was also used when going on holiday: in the summer of 1958 it even took Donald, Gwen, Donald's mother, Ruth and Peter to Hopeman in the north east of Scotland. However, there was no doubt that it was an old car, so the young folk in the church decided to have a bit of fun and, much to Donald's delight, put a sticker on the back of the car which read 'Don't rock around this old crock!' Eventually, when Donald was kindly gifted a more modern car he gave the Austin 7 to the minister in Islay.

From the beginning of his ministry in Stirling, Donald showed his ability to connect with young people, both inside and outside of the church. There was already a good Sunday School in the church, led by Jack Adam, with the youngest children meeting during the morning service and the older children (the junior Sunday School) meeting immediately after the service. After a few years there were Sunday School camps in the summer and Donald went to two of them, in Arran and in Islay.

Donald started a Bible Class for young people, taking place at the same time as the junior Sunday School. Tea and biscuits were provided in the church kitchen after the morning service for those waiting on to Sunday School or Bible Class – a very necessary provision for Donald, as his diabetes meant that he had to eat at regular intervals and he would not be home for his Sunday lunch until at least 2pm. The Bible Class was soon established and grew steadily under the leadership of Tom Ferguson. The younger children were not forgotten, with the formation of a Life Boy team to supplement the active Boys' Brigade which was already part of church life.

The Youth Fellowship was also growing, both in numbers and in enthusiasm. In the early years of Donald's ministry a space underneath the church building was used as a paint-shop, but when the painters retired the youth group decided to clean it out so that they could make use of it. Donald was keen to see the space used as a café for young folk who would not be interested in coming into the church building for a service, but would be happy enough to come into the informal atmosphere of a café. After a lot of hard work by the church young people, the café – named 'The Dugout' - was ready. It was open every Wednesday evening and became very successful. Members of the Youth Fellowship went out into the streets of Stirling, armed with a questionnaire prepared by Donald. This questionnaire was used as an opening for conversation before an invitation to the café was given. Once in the café, there were tables laid out where people could chat informally, as well as a more formal session each evening where guests were invited to ask questions about the Christian faith.

In addition to the Youth Fellowship on a Sunday evening and the cafe each Wednesday, there were sometimes youth meetings on a Saturday night, organised by the Stirling and Clackmannanshire Baptist Association. On one occasion when Donald accompanied a group of young people to one of these meetings, they were all waiting for a bus when another group of young folk came up to the bus stop and roughly pushed their way to the front of the queue. Donald, angry at their rudeness, remonstrated with them, but one lad lashed out, causing Donald's mouth to bleed badly. By the time he reached home his face was very swollen.

Donald willingly gave himself for others, but others were also involved in giving sacrificially of their time and energy. On one occasion, after visiting a family in the Raploch area of Stirling, Donald asked members of the Youth Fellowship to do a very unpleasant task. Walking through the close to visit the family in their flat he had been horrified and upset, for the close walls were smeared with blood. Somebody had been murdered in the close and no-one had cleaned the blood away. Always concerned for people's welfare, Donald asked if some members of the Youth Fellowship would clean up the close and so help the family. They willingly did as he asked, but found it a most unpleasant experience. Islwyn Williams, who was in charge of the cleaning operation, said that it was a horrible job and remarked,

"I have a good appetite, but when I went home that night I wasn't hungry!"

The Youth Fellowship continued to grow steadily during the time of Donald's ministry in Stirling. In the mid 1960s a church member who was a music teacher, May Lewis, decided that there were enough young people to form a good sized choir. She began choir practices and gave the choir a name - 'The Pioneers'. Although most of the young folk had had no previous musical training, she managed to teach them so well that they were able to take on engagements throughout Scotland. Most of their music was composed by May herself. The Youth Fellowship, to Donald's delight, was now reaching out not only to the young people of Stirling, but well beyond the boundaries of the town.

While in Granton, Donald had enjoyed being chaplain to the local secondary school, Ainsley Park.

He was therefore delighted when in the early 1960s the opportunity arose to be chaplain of Riverside Secondary School in Stirling. For a number of years he took a weekly service in the school and in 1965 he started a Scripture Union group. After the group had been meeting for a few months he invited them to go along to a baptismal service in Stirling Baptist Church. One of the group – Linda Watts – took up the invitation to attend. Recalling that night she said:

"I was really impressed by the service and whatever these people had, I wanted. At the close of the service there was an appeal and I went forward. That night was the beginning of my walk with the Lord and not too long afterwards I was baptised myself by Mr McCallum."

A number of years later Linda lived in Wigtown in Dumfries and Galloway, where she became a founder member of Wigtown Baptist Church.

As early as April 1958, Donald's burning desire to see the young people of Scotland committed to the cause of Christ was apparent in a contribution to the Scottish Baptist Magazine, a magazine to which he regularly contributed. Perhaps inspired by the gift of a picture portraying Jesus and his disciples as young men – a picture which hung in his study for the rest of his life - he challenged the young Baptists of Scotland to think about the quality of their youth group and to notice

"that Jesus was a young man when he died, that the first disciples were young men, and that the first Christian fellowship was, quite literally, a youth fellowship."

Later that year, the Baptist Union of Scotland recognised Donald's ability by appointing him Convenor of the Young People's Committee, a post he held until

1964. These were incredibly busy years, ministering to a growing church in Stirling as well as overseeing the work with the young Baptists of Scotland.

In January 1959 Donald used the regular slot in the Scottish Baptist magazine, 'Accent on Youth', to introduce himself as the new Youth Convenor and to set the young Baptists of Scotland a challenge:

"Youth is the time for SERVICE – when we feel the urge, indeed necessity, to give ourselves to some great cause, or for some great ideal . . There are many claimants for the service of youth, but no claim is so valid as Christ's. . . Youth is the time for SACRIFICE, for giving oneself away for some cause which seems greater than life itself."

Over the next few years, Donald regularly wrote to the young Baptists of Scotland through 'Accent on Youth', passionately urging them to give their all for the sake of Christ.

He also used the magazine to inform them of forthcoming events. In April 1959 he expressed a desire to have the young Baptists of Scotland meet together and informed them that he was in the process of arranging a conference and rally in Stirling on Saturday 30th May. Details of the conference were given and an offer of hospitality was made for those who would find it difficult to come to Stirling and return home on the same day. In May 1959 he again encouraged young people to come:

"This is the first Youth Conference and Rally of its kind; it should help to bring us all together – enable us to learn together and discover ways of working together. Pray for its success – and be present if you can."

The Youth Conference and Rally were successful beyond anyone's wildest dreams! Members of the

Stirling church willingly provided help to make the day a success: food was ordered and served, the caretaker's garden behind the Baptist church was set with tables, people were welcomed as they arrived and many other essential organisational tasks were carried out with energy and good humour. The numbers at the event surpassed all expectations, with the church full for the afternoon conference and overflowing for the evening rally – young people seated in the choir area, the doorways, the window sills, the aisles and even the baptistry! One of the Stirling young people – Jean Lewis – welcomed everyone to this first Scottish Baptist Youth Conference and Rally. Overwhelmed by the number of young people around him, the speaker for the evening – Mr Lindsay Glegg – began his address by expressing his delight at being there, "knee-deep in Baptists!"

The Youth Rally at the Baptist Union of Scotland Assembly in October of that year was also very well attended. A report on the rally in the December 1959 Scottish Baptist magazine recorded that

"some of the young men had to sit on the pulpit steps while the chairman, Rev. D. P. McCallum, of Stirling, kept urging those seated to "Squeeze in another inch."!"

The runaway success of the May conference and rally encouraged Donald to organise a similar event for the following May. He began informing the young people of Scotland about arrangements in the January edition of the Scottish Baptist magazine, but this time there was to be something more. Always concerned for those who lived away from the central belt of Scotland, Donald stated,

". . we would like to organise rallies at about the same

time in areas too far away from the centre to participate in the larger one."

Areas interested in this idea were asked to contact Donald himself, and thus began the rallies in the north east of Scotland, immediately before or after the May conference and rally.

The speaker for the 1960 rally was Rev. Tom Allan of Glasgow, while at the afternoon conference Rev. T. J. Daries of York spoke on the gospel of John. Young folk were asked to prepare for the afternoon by studying set texts from the gospel and to be prepared to take part in group discussions. Once again the conference and rally attracted large numbers, but this time the North Parish church, next door to the Baptist church in Stirling and the biggest suitable building in the town, was used for the occasion. This bigger church was filled almost to capacity for the evening rally, with approximately nine hundred attending. The afternoon speaker was well received, although it was agreed that the group sizes were too big for meaningful discussion. The evening rally was, however, deemed to be excellent. Members and friends of Stirling Baptist Church once again willingly helped to make the day a success, thrilled at the numbers attending and the sense of excitement among the young people of Scotland. Catering for such large numbers was no easy task: so many people came that the teas had to be served in several sessions!

These Youth rallies continued to grow. In May 1961 almost one thousand young people attended the rally where the speaker was Sven Ohm from Sweden, the Secretary of the European Baptist Federation. Thrilled at the continuing success of the rallies, Donald wrote about

Sven Ohm's address in the July 1961 Scottish Baptist magazine:

"We caught a vision of the great Baptist family to which we belong, and, I believe, a vision of the Christ who was present in the midst, challenging us all to deeper consecration and endeavour."

The May 1962 rally, addressed by Dr Erik Ruden, Eastern Secretary of the Baptist World Alliance, filled the North Church in Stirling to capacity, squeezing in an estimated 1200 people, with more than half the Baptist Churches in Scotland represented, quite apart from those who went to the Northern Rally in Elgin. There were also visitors from the North of England, U.S.A., Jamaica and Sierra Leone. The afternoon conference was also well attended, when - in a new format called "Two men open the Bible" - Rev. Peter Barber questioned Rev. Jim Taylor about Baptist principles. To an already packed programme, one more event was added - a News Session was fitted in between the afternoon and evening sessions.

It was obvious that these rallies had caught the imagination of the young Baptists of Scotland. In the July 1962 edition of the Scottish Baptist magazine, Donald commented:

"I am hoping that something has begun in each young heart as a result of these wonderful gatherings – something which will be worked out in our lives, our homes and our churches."

The 1963 conference and rally attracted even more and by 1964 the number of young people coming was so great that the North Church in Stirling could no longer cope. The venue, instead, was the Church of

Scotland Assembly Hall in Edinburgh which had 2000 seats. Donald had high hopes for this event, writing to young people in the April edition of the Scottish Baptist magazine:

"If the Holy Spirit falls upon this great gathering in convicting power, and inspires all these young people with love for the Lord and zeal for His Gospel, it could be the turning of the spiritual tide in our land."

More than 1700 people attended an inspiring rally where the first full-time Director of Christian Education and Youth Work for Scottish Baptists was commissioned – Rev. G. H. Ritchie. The Youth Work had grown so much under Donald's guidance that it was no longer possible for one man to combine a pastoral ministry and the work of Youth Convenor. Donald's time as Youth Convenor had come to an end. In an emotional farewell after a slot entitled 'Donald McCallum, This is Your Life!' a member of the Stirling congregation presented him with a gift on behalf of the young people of the Scottish Baptist churches.

The Youth Rallies, however, had been only a small part of the work in which Donald had engaged as Youth Convenor. In 1961 he arranged the first Continental holiday for Scottish Baptist young people – a trip to Holland by bus to stay in the Dutch Baptist Youth Centre, 'De Vinkenhof'. All the arrangements were made through the Stirling Travel Agent in Friar's Street and buses were hired from the Stirling bus garage in Riverside.

The response to the holiday was immediate: within a fortnight, all the accommodation was fully booked and an offer was then made of tents in the grounds of 'De

Vinkenhof' for some of the young men. This, too, was taken up and in the end seventy young people went to Holland in new buses which, unfortunately, turned out to have one fault – the heating could not be switched off! Nevertheless, the young people had a wonderful time: visits to places of interest in Holland, a trip to Cologne in Germany, Sunday worship with Dutch Baptists and inspiring conference sessions led by Rev. Peter Barber.

This first holiday was such a success that Donald tried to arrange a similar holiday in Sweden for the following year. He was unsuccessful in doing this, but instead was given the offer of accommodation in a new Baptist Centre – 'Greenhills' in Worthing. This turned out to be another memorable holiday, with many young Scottish Baptists appreciating the fun and fellowship as well as a visit to London and parts of the south of England. Donald arranged one more holiday just before relinquishing the post of Youth Convenor: a second trip to 'De Vinkenhof' in Holland, this time by train and with a smaller party. All these holidays were greatly appreciated, beginning at a time when few Scottish young people went abroad.

At the same time, Donald continued to organise the regular autumn conferences for young Baptists at 'Piersland' in Troon as well as one or two conferences at Gean House in Alloa. Jean Lewis, a member of the Stirling church, acted as his unofficial secretary for all these events. On one occasion Donald, Jean and some others were returning to Stirling in Donald's car after a conference when heavy snow started to fall. At that point they were on the outskirts of Glasgow but had twenty-six more miles to cover before reaching Stirling. Unfortunately the windscreen wipers suddenly stopped working. Jean was sitting in the front passenger seat, so Donald informed her that the wipers could be worked manually by a switch just in front of her.

"If you want us to get home tonight, you'll have to work the wipers!" he exclaimed.

By the time they all reached Stirling Jean's hand felt as if it was about to fall off, but they all reached home safely.

Another member of the church, Betty Lauder, provided Donald with invaluable secretarial help. Her typing skills were put to good use helping Donald cope with the mountain of mail which came to the manse during his time as Youth Convenor. Betty joked that coping with Donald's correspondence kept her busier than her day job in the civil service! Donald happily admitted that his writing could be almost unreadable and his typing with two fingers not much better, so he was very grateful for Betty's skills and the speed with which she was able to complete the letters. Such willing practical support from a number of Stirling church members freed Donald to focus on his work as Youth Convenor.

Another innovation during Donald's time as Youth Convenor was a paper called 'The Fiery Cross', first published in October 1961 by an editorial team composed of three young people from Fife, Glasgow and Edinburgh, giving detailed information of what was happening among young Scottish Baptists. A picture of Donald was on the front page of the first edition, accompanying an article entitled 'Something is happening!' where he explained:

"This paper is making its appearance when things are happening among the young Baptists of Scotland. I wonder if we are aware of what is taking place?"

He urged young people to take note of the contents of the paper as

"All these happenings should command our prayers and our intelligent participation. God is at work and we are workers together with Him."

The paper was published quarterly for several years.

In addition to organising rallies and conferences, planning holidays, writing for the Scottish Baptist magazine and helping to launch 'The Fiery Cross', Donald regularly accepted invitations to speak at young people's meetings around Scotland in addition to speaking at some in England. He particularly enjoyed speaking to students in the colleges and universities as well as his visits to young people in the remoter parts of Scotland, as he knew first-hand the particular difficulties experienced by those who could not easily come to events in central Scotland.

All these activities linked to the post of Youth Convenor, added to the responsibilities he had as pastor of the church in Stirling, meant that Donald was exceptionally busy. He readily admitted that it was Gwen's constant loving help and support that allowed him to achieve as much as he did. Many years later he commented: "Gwen effectively brought up the two children while I pastored the church and was Youth Convenor for the Baptist Union. Through this period I was extremely busy."

One of the most significant events in the life of Stirling Baptist Church during this time was the beginning of work in the Cornton area of the town where a lot of council housing was being built during the 1950s. No church had been built in the area, so the Baptist Church applied for permission to hold a Sunday School in the community hall. The Youth Fellowship and some other church members visited all the houses in Cornton to tell them about the start of the Sunday School and then went round with reminders in the week before the first meeting. On the day, Sunday 22nd November 1959, more than one hundred children turned up!   Within two months the Sunday School was well established, with both a primary and a junior section, ably led by a deacon appointed by Stirling Baptist Church, Jim Galloway. He and his wife, Ruth, went on to give many years of unstinting service to the work in Cornton.

The Community Hall was in poor condition, but over the next few years it was well used, with a successful Girls Life Brigade Company starting in 1963 and, for a short time, a women's meeting. It was very clear that the building had a limited lifespan, so it was no surprise to find that it was due for demolition, along with the last of the post-war prefabs in the area. The church, which had already been considering building a hall in Cornton, was advised that land was available provided there was enough money to pay for the construction of a building.

At that time, the Youth Fellowship had a fund which contained the princely sum of £47. They were willing to give the money they had saved, but the new hall had to be in place within a year and was going to cost much more than £47! Nothing daunted, Donald said,

"The Lord will provide!"

and the church agreed to go ahead, having plans drawn up for the construction of a hall and then putting the job out to tender. By the time this was done, the Youth Fellowship fund had grown to £100, but much more was needed. One of the church deacons confessed,

"I was worried, but Donald wasn't. He was sure the Lord would provide."

In spite of this conviction, Donald was astonished when an elderly lady, a member of Stirling Baptist Church, phoned him one day to say that she would like to pay for the new hall! She wanted to remain anonymous at that time, but was willing for her name to be associated with the gift after her death. The lady was Isa Neilson, who had become a Christian at the Billy Graham Crusade in 1955. After coming to live in Kippen, near Stirling, she had been baptised in Stirling Baptist Church at the age of 70. On the day she phoned Donald she had just inherited a large sum of money after the death of her sister. She wanted to give the money to support the church's work in Cornton because of her desire to see the outreach work prosper but also because of her particular interest in the area: she had been brought up on the land where the prefabs had been built. As money became available she kept giving it to the church and, when the final amount was handed over, it was enough to pay not only for the completion of the building but also for a set of hymnbooks. Donald had been quite correct: The Lord did provide, right down to the practicalities of hymnbooks for the first morning service!

In February 1966 the foundation stone for the building was laid, with the official opening in September of that same year. Gwen was given the privilege of cutting the ribbon and declaring the building open. As she did this she declared,

"This is the story of the beginnings of a work of God, but many chapters have yet to be written. May the present be worthy of the past and may the future eclipse them both."

The very next day the first Sunday morning service in Cornton took place. There was now a suitable building, with a seating capacity of 250, for all the activities which had taken place in the old community hall as well as for a new Sunday service of worship.

While Donald was occupied with all the work which a thriving church brings, Gwen led a busy life too: keeping a large house clean and tidy, looking after the family, carefully watching over Donald to ensure that his diabetes was well controlled, leading the Women's Auxiliary (a weekly meeting for women in the church), hosting a monthly gathering for ministers' wives and entertaining the many visitors to the manse. Gwen was famed for her baking, as she would regularly give Donald a freshly-baked gingerbread to take to people he was visiting. Donald often said,

"These gingerbreads do more good than my sermons!"

When visitors came to the manse for a meal or for a longer stay they would comment on the mouth-watering array of baking on the table – and over the years there were many visitors from all around the world. Missionaries were frequent visitors, often in the middle of a speaking tour around the country, telling churches about their work. Many missionaries would arrive at the manse looking very tired, but after Gwen's ministrations they would leave refreshed. One lady arrived at the manse door looking absolutely exhausted and Gwen's first words to her were,

"Would you like a bath?"

Donald was highly amused at this and often teased Gwen about it afterwards, but the bath was just what was needed to allow the lady to relax. One missionary enjoyed joining in a Sunday School picnic to Doune; another missionary was diabetic and was relieved to be in a household where a diabetic's needs were so well understood; many simply appreciated the peace and quiet of a room in the large house.

Speakers at the various Youth Rallies visited the manse, most memorably two Russian pastors during the era of the Cold War, as well as many other people from around the world. For a number of years, American choirs made regular visits to Scotland. The choir would give a concert in the church and then be given hospitality in church members' homes. Needless to say, the manse was one of the homes to be used for such hospitality. As a result of all these visitors, discussions around the tea table were wide ranging and the whole family appreciated the insights from the many guests who had a meal in the manse. There were amusing incidents too, such as the time when a rather large American visitor sat down on a chair which promptly broke underneath him!

If people were staying for a few days, Gwen liked to introduce them to the delights of Stirling and the surrounding countryside. She took many visitors to Stirling Castle, the Wallace Monument, the Trossachs and, her favourite place, the Lake of Mentieth. Donald was usually too busy to accompany her on these outings and it was a standing joke in the family that he never went up the Wallace Monument in spite of living near it for many years.

In the autumn of 1958, Ruth's best friend, Glenys Hill, came to stay at the manse. Ruth was, needless to say, very excited but the circumstances which led to this were tragic. Glenys' mother had been diagnosed with cancer and had to go into the Stirling Infirmary for surgery, followed by treatment in Glasgow. As Glenys' father worked some distance away from Stirling, he had to leave home early in the morning, but knew that his daughter was much too young to be left alone to get up and go to school by herself. After speaking to Donald and Gwen it was arranged that Glenys would stay at the manse from a Sunday evening until a Friday evening while her mother was in hospital, returning home to her father at weekends. Sadly, Mrs Hill was in hospital on several occasions over the next two and a half years, before her death in the early summer of 1961. On each occasion, Glenys would come to stay and her father would arrive at the manse every evening to see Glenys, after visiting his wife in hospital. After her mother's death Glenys continued to stay at the manse during the week, going to school each day with Ruth, until she was old enough to be left on her own before and after school. This was a very sad time, but deep and lasting ties of friendship were made between the two families.

A number of other friends and family members stayed in the manse for varying periods of time. In 1960 Donald's sister and brother-in-law, Ruby and Willie Dudgeon, went to India for four years to work in Dr. Graham's Homes in Kalimpong. Their elder daughter, Kathleen, had to return to the UK a year before the rest of her family to complete her schooling so she stayed at the manse and attended Stirling High School. Donald and Gwen were delighted to have an extended family and, thankfully, the house was large enough to easily accommodate everyone. Then when Ruby, Willie and their younger daughter, Moira, returned to Scotland, they too stayed in the manse until they were able to find a home of their own.

Meanwhile, the church was continuing to grow under Donald's leadership. His passion for evangelism led to many forms of outreach as well as a desire to see members of the congregation grow in their faith. In late 1967, Donald introduced the Christian Training programme to the church. Over a period of eleven weeks, a course based on the letter of James was offered in order to help church members apply their Christian faith to their daily lives. The course took place on two evenings each week to allow parents of young children to attend. On the first week of the course, Rev. R.E.O. White gave an introduction to the letter, but other evenings had a different structure: lesson outlines were prepared by Donald, who opened each evening by summarising the topic for the evening; thereafter, there was group discussion on questions prepared by Donald, then prayer within each group before all groups came together for a time of worship at the conclusion of the evening. Course notes, typed by Betty Lauder, were available each week. One hundred and eighteen people enrolled for the course and were so appreciative that a second course was immediately planned for the following spring.

By this time, Baptismal services were taking place frequently, often with a large number of people of varying ages being baptised. These services were inspirational, with the church building often packed to capacity. One Baptismal service regularly led to another and there was a sense of excitement about what God was doing in Stirling Baptist Church at that time, a time when many churches throughout Scotland were experiencing a fall in attendance and membership. Donald later described these years as a time when there was a "mini revival".

Donald's preaching gift continued to develop, with the result that many people came to services to hear him preach. These sermons were the result of much preparation: Donald spent a good deal of time each week preparing his sermons, coming up with imaginative titles, such as 'The men who never died'. Always thinking ahead, he made a point of advertising the title of forthcoming sermons in the local weekly newspaper – The Stirling Observer. At the end of a service he regularly made an appeal for people in the congregation to commit their lives to Christ. He expected a response and on many occasions did see people openly commit themselves to Christian faith. Two of these people were nurses who had come to work in Stirling Royal Infirmary.

The first of these was a young woman who had come to Stirling to do a midwifery course. She had been involved in a church before coming to Stirling but had not made any particular commitment as a Christian. One Sunday morning she arrived at Stirling Baptist Church for the first time and was captivated by the service and the sermon. When Donald asked if anyone in the congregation would like to become a Christian she immediately responded. A few weeks later she was baptised and joined the church. This young woman, Nettie Sinclair, went on to give forty years' Christian service in Kenya with the Africa Inland Mission.

The second young nurse, Barbara Wrightson, came from London. Before leaving London, one of her friends had asked her to go to church but she had not done so.

She felt that she had let her friend down so on the first morning she was in Stirling she set out to find a church. As she walked from the hospital into the town she noticed a man with a Bible and asked if he knew of a church to which she could go. Although the man did not attend the Baptist church he directed her there saying,

"Look lassie, I think you'll be more at home there."

She went in and before long she became a Christian and was baptised. When she became a Christian she was so excited by the Bible that she read it just like a daily newspaper!

Later on she went to the Northern Territory of Australia to work with the Maoris.

Throughout this time Donald continued to play an active role in the affairs of the Baptist Union of Scotland. Although no longer Youth Convenor, he continued to give support to Youth work, such as his involvement in the visit to Scotland in May 1965 of three Russian pastors, one of whom – Rev. Michael Zhidkov of Moscow Baptist Church – spoke at the May Youth rally that year. In addition, he was nominated for the position of President of the Baptist Union of Scotland - a role which would involve him in a good deal of committee work and visiting of churches over a period of three years, as vice-president, president and then past president. He allowed his name to go forward for this position, with the result that at the Baptist Union of Scotland Assembly in October 1965 he was appointed Vice-President.

Donald at the beginning of his Presidential year

Throughout his vice-presidential year he was busy, travelling to Glasgow for committees and visiting a number of churches throughout Scotland as well as continuing to look after the church in Stirling. On the Sunday before taking up the role of President of the Baptist Union of Scotland, BBC Radio Scotland came to Stirling Baptist Church to transmit a live broadcast of the morning service. During the service Donald preached on the 23rd Psalm. The sermon obviously touched many people for he received a large number of letters from all over Scotland, thanking him for what he had said. Donald replied to each one of these letters, dictating most of the replies to Betty Lauder, who then typed them.

"Letters came cascading in," said Betty. "People were so appreciative of the excellent message."

One letter Donald received at this time had a particular significance for him: the Headmaster of Boroughmuir School in Edinburgh sent his congratulations on Donald's appointment as President. Always exceedingly proud to be a former pupil of the school, Donald was delighted to receive the letter but unfortunately was too busy to take up the invitation of a visit to the school.

The Assembly of the Baptist Union of Scotland in October 1966, held in the Church of Scotland Assembly Rooms in Edinburgh, was the beginning of Donald's Presidential year, an exceptionally busy and very exciting time for him. His Presidential Address, entitled 'New Wine . . . and Old Bottles', was a passionate declaration of his belief in the power of the Gospel:

"The Gospel is New Wine from the blood stained vintage of Calvary, and when fermented by a living faith, and sparkling with the energy of the Holy Spirit, it is a life-

changing, world-shattering force. It is spiritual dynamite, the channel of the energy of God."

This declaration was accompanied by a plea for Christians to look for new ways of presenting the Gospel while avoiding the use of gimmicks to simply attract attention.

"New Wine needs new bottles. Patterns of thinking, living and giving must stretch, if the New Wine of the gospel is to be offered to this generation."

His passionate address was well received, with printed copies selling out very quickly. However, Donald was desperate to see his presidential address translated into action and throughout his year of office he encouraged the Baptists of Scotland to do just that.

As President, he was invited to speak in Baptist churches over the length and breadth of Scotland, but this meant that during his Presidential year he was preaching in his own church only once a month and he was often away from home. Although his life was very busy, he loved visiting other churches to bring them encouragement and challenge, regularly writing articles about these visits in the Scottish Baptist Magazine in order to inform others of his travels .

He was particularly impressed by his visits to Orkney, Shetland and the island of Tiree. Writing in the magazine about his time in Orkney and Shetland, he described places and journeys in detail, as well as calling it *". . one of my most interesting, and spiritually rewarding, presidential journeys."* In the article on Orkney, entitled 'Beyond the Barriers' he gave details of his visit to Kirkwall and then Westray which had reinforced his belief that small churches mattered:

"Neither Westray nor Kirkwall boast large populations, by mainland standards. But we must not let mere size or numbers blind us to more important factors or cause us to neglect the work of God in smaller communities."

He was challenged by what he saw of the church in Kirkwall which had recently acquired a church building and a manse, stating, *"All this rebukes my own coldness and challenges my faith."* He was also thrilled and intrigued to be taken to Westray by Jack Scott, a member of the Westray church, in a boat which he had built himself. Although not the best of sailors, Donald thoroughly enjoyed the experience, talking about it for many years afterwards.

The visit to Shetland was equally exciting and challenging. As well as preaching in Lerwick, he was given a civic reception in the town before going on to visit churches in Dunrossness and Burra Isle. He felt greatly privileged to preach in these three churches *"and was tremendously impressed by the vigour and quality of spiritual life among them."* While visiting the homes of some members of the Sandsting and Lunnasting churches he was deeply moved by the devotion of one young woman who had come many miles in order to be able to attend a meeting in a croft house. After the meeting, Donald was in a car which took her as far as possible towards her home, but she had to

"walk the remaining miles to her home over a track which would un-nerve a townsman by day, but she did it at night."

Commenting on this, Donald observed,

"It makes some of our reasons for non-attendance at worship or the prayer meeting seem kind of empty, doesn't it?"

Writing about his visit to Tiree, Donald confessed to being so thrilled to arrive on the island that he managed to leave his case at the airport! Fortunately, he managed to retrieve the case from the airport manager who, by the time Donald caught up with him, was on his croft making hay. Donald then spent a busy weekend on the island, visiting church members and preaching at church services.

Throughout his presidential year, Donald chaired many Baptist Union committees in Glasgow. This meant that he was regularly away from home during the week as well as preaching all over Scotland on three out of every four Sundays. When his Presidential year came to an end he was very glad to be at home again with his family and with the church family in Stirling. Eager to inform the church members of his travels as President, he arranged an evening when he showed some slides and talked about his 'Presidential Peregrinations'.

In late 1967 Donald accepted the post of chairmanship of the Scottish Churches' Council Evangelism Committee. He had always had a passion for evangelism and a willingness to work with the different church denominations in Scotland for the purpose of reaching Scotland for Christ. This was obvious in an article he wrote for the Scottish Baptist Magazine about his visit to the islands of Islay and Colonsay in December 1966. As well as preaching in the Baptist Churches of both islands and visiting people in their homes, while on Colonsay he also spent time in the island school and attended a Sunday School in the Parish Church which was led by a member of the Baptist Church! He was pleased to see the way the churches were working together on the island, noting that

"Both churches retain their identity and character, but have also found a way of expressing their fellowship in Christ."

Even when on holiday, Donald was thinking about evangelism! While in a caravan on Skye in the summer of 1967, he wrote a passionate article which was later published in the Scottish Baptist magazine. In it he revealed his desire to see Scotland evangelised, with churches working together for that one purpose. He made it absolutely clear that he did not favour the idea of all church denominations uniting in a National Church. Instead, he fervently desired

"to be on terms with all our brethren in Christ of any and every denomination, and to consult with them and work with them in Christian courtesy and love."

He saw Scotland in 1967 as an exciting, challenging place in which to be a Christian, urging all Baptists to practise

". . personal holiness, thoroughly responsible churchmanship and a passion to make Christ known."

In May 1968 Donald was involved in organising a Conference on Evangelism which took place in Stirling High School. As part of the conference, one thousand people took part in a march from the gates of the King's Park to the town's Albert Hall where a rally was held. The residents of Stirling could not ignore the presence of so many people intent on evangelising Scotland!

In 1969 it was Gwen's turn to hold a national position when she was elected as President of the Women's Auxiliary to the Baptist Union of Scotland during the Union's centenary year. As a very busy minister's wife, the theme for her Presidential address reflected her practice over many years: "They that wait upon the Lord shall renew their strength." During her year as President, she needed that strength as she travelled the length and breadth of Scotland. Always a 'home bird', she became known for her desire, wherever possible, to return home at the end of a meeting rather than have overnight hospitality! In this, she was not only considering her own needs but also those of Donald who depended greatly on Gwen's medical skills to help keep his diabetes on an even keel, often publicly acknowledging his reliance on his "own wee nurse".

As well as the usual responsibilities as President, Gwen was also invited to give a series of talks about prayer on 'Late Call', a programme on STV. She had been on the Women's World Day of Prayer Committee and was asked to take part in that capacity. This was a very exciting opportunity, involving a day at the STV studios and then transmission of the programmes at a later date. Gwen spent much time considering what to say on each evening, but a conversation soon after the transmission of the programmes had the family laughing heartily: a young woman told Gwen how much she and her husband had enjoyed all the talks then added her husband's remark, "Mrs. McCallum must have been a good looking woman once!"

Meanwhile, as Donald and Gwen's ministry continued to expand, the town of Stirling was changing. At the beginning of their ministry in 1956 it had been very much a traditional market town serving a farming community, with sheep still occasionally being driven in from outlying farms through the centre of the town to the mart. Soon after arriving in Stirling, Ruth clearly remembers Gwen shouting to her,

"Come to the front door and see this!"

When she looked out of the door, there was a flock of sheep walking down Albert Place on their way into the centre of the town and to the mart which was then situated in Riverside. By the 1960s, however, all animal transport was motorised and the town had expanded considerably.

One of the biggest changes came in 1967 when Stirling University opened its doors to students for the first time. Donald became one of the first chaplains to the University, a post which astonished him greatly as he himself had not had the opportunity to go to university! However, his gift for working with young people ensured that he was able to make a significant contribution to the beginnings of the chaplaincy in Stirling University.

While busy with all the work of the church in Stirling and around Scotland, Donald was becoming restless. He was convinced that his time in Stirling was coming to an end, so spent much time in prayer about the next move. After so many happy years in Stirling it was a wrench to move away, but when the call came from Adelaide Place Baptist Church in the centre of Glasgow, Donald was utterly convinced that this was a call from God, one he had been sensing in his spirit for some time. After an emotional farewell to the many friends in Stirling, Donald's ministry there came to an end in January 1970.

The years in Stirling had been very busy but on the whole very happy ones for the family. During these years Ruth and Peter grew from children into young adults, enjoying life at school, in the church and in the community. Both were baptised by Donald and joined the church. By the time Donald accepted the call to Adelaide Place, Ruth was a student at Edinburgh University and Peter was working in Glasgow.

There had been two sad family events in the early years: Gwen had one more miscarriage and then Donald's mother died in December 1958. She had been ill for much of the time since the move from Edinburgh but, thankfully, had been able to attend church and make a few friends. In January 1959 the 'In Memoriam' section of The Scottish Baptist Magazine recorded her death and commented:

"Our friend was clothed with the loveliness and the gentleness of her Saviour, whose grace and graces were manifest in her life and character."

Gwen's own ministry, exercised in so many different ways, had fully supported all that Donald had done. Every single day Gwen kept a close eye on Donald's health, for he often drove himself to the limit of his physical strength, regularly suffering from a 'hypo' when he needed to consume something sweet to raise his blood sugar. Many members and friends of the Stirling church could recognise the symptoms of a 'hypo' and would provide assistance when necessary. Just after Donald had accepted the call to Adelaide Place he went to visit one of the church members who lived in Stirling. On the way to the house he began to need sugar and was quite disorientated. Donald was so well known in the town that a neighbour of the church member recognised him and took him to the member's house where he was given a cup of sweet tea which soon revived him.

For most of the time in Stirling, Gwen had to work hard to look after a large house as well as a growing family and many visitors. Once a week one of the church members came to help clean, but it was still a big task. In 1968 the church deacons recognised that the manse needed considerable upgrading, so it was sold and a more compact and warmer house was bought, appropriately, in Manse Crescent. Gwen had only eighteen months in this house of her dreams before she moved to Glasgow.

The years in Stirling Baptist Church had been very fruitful, with the church growing from just over 200 members in 1956 to well over 300 in 1970. In addition, Donald had also been able to exercise a ministry throughout Scotland. It would have been easy to stay in a church which was growing but Donald was looking for a challenge and he was totally convinced that the challenge lay in Glasgow city centre. When one heartbroken member of the Stirling church asked why he was going away he replied,

"I couldn't face the Lord if I didn't accept this call."

New challenges lay ahead, but the friendships made during the years in Stirling were strong. Although Donald and Gwen were sad to move away from such loving and supportive people, they looked forward with anticipation to the future.

Chapter 9

Adelaide Place, Glasgow: a city centre church

Donald's ministry in Adelaide Place Baptist Church began on Saturday 7th February 1970, just after his 53rd birthday, when the service of induction took place. Three of Donald's friends from the Baptist Union of Scotland took part in the induction– Rev. Peter Barber, the President of the Union, Rev. George Hossack, the ex-President, and Rev. James Taylor. Another friend, Rev. Andrew MacRae, the Secretary of the Baptist Union, took part in the Welcome Social which was held in the evening. The March edition of the Scottish Baptist Magazine reported on the weekend's celebrations, noting that

" . the church greets his coming with eager anticipation, confident that Adelaide Place still has a vital role to play in the mission field in the city centre."

By the end of the weekend at least one of the church members knew that Donald would waste no time in finding out what that role was. Bill Dougall was welcoming visitors to the Induction Service when a member of Stirling Baptist Church stood aside from the crowd and remarked,

"You'll never manage to keep him down. You'll have to sit on him!"

It was not long before the congregation in Adelaide Place found that remark to be absolutely true!

From the start, Donald was excited about the challenges which lay ahead. Totally convinced that God had called him to Glasgow, he set about facing the demanding situations presented by a city centre ministry. The first difficulty to be overcome was a very practical one – the task of finding a suitable manse. Adelaide Place already had a manse in the Kelvindale area of the city, but Donald was looking for a house much nearer to the church. He wanted to be closer to the centre of the city, where people were, so that he would be more accessible for anyone who needed help. He also wanted a large house which could easily accommodate visitors as well as the family.

For the first four months of their ministry in Glasgow, Donald and Gwen continued to live in the Stirling manse, travelling to Glasgow almost daily for meetings and for pastoral work. Each Sunday different members of the congregation gave the family hospitality for the day, a kindness which turned out to be a good way of meeting many of the people who attended services on a Sunday.

During these months the church deacons looked at several houses before finding a large town house in Holyrood Crescent, close to Kelvinbridge and near the city centre. The house was large, with plenty of room for the family and the anticipated visitors; the city centre was within walking distance; but best of all, as far as Donald was concerned, there was a large room on the first floor whose walls were lined with bookshelves! This became Donald's study, with books from floor to ceiling on three of the four walls. The house had previously belonged to the Chief Rabbi in Glasgow who had obviously loved books and Donald was only too pleased to inherit such a magnificent study.

Donald at the beginning of his ministry in Adelaide Place Baptist Church

However, the rest of the family was not quite so delighted. After living on the outskirts of Stirling for most of their lives, Ruth and Peter were horrified at the house's proximity to the centre of the city, the enormous size and the poor state of interior decoration. On their first visit to 4 Holyrood Crescent they picnicked in the lounge with Donald and Gwen, resting their cups on the decaying mantelpiece, surrounded by peeling wallpaper and wishing that a better house had been found!. A tour of the rest of the house simply confirmed their horror: the interior decoration was sadly in need of a complete make-over and Ruth and Peter wondered if it could ever be made habitable.

In complete contrast to his family, Donald could see only the positive signs, encouraging them to understand the reasons for buying such a house so close to the city centre. The members of the Adelaide Place congregation, on the other hand, were much more understanding of Donald's desire for a large house in a central location, rising to the challenge and engaging a firm to decorate it from top to bottom. Donald even chose paper for the large hallway and, much to the surprise of his family, picked colours and paper which suited the hall very well! Carpets, too, were renewed. As the work proceeded, one of the deacons, Campbell McKinnon, kept urging the family to imagine the house in good repair. Eventually the re-decoration and refurbishment were finished, transforming the large house into a warm, welcoming manse.

Gwen then had to cope with the upheaval of a house removal during her busy year as President of the Women's Auxiliary to the Baptist Union of Scotland. In June 1970 she left behind her dream house in Stirling and soon made the refurbished Holyrood Crescent house into a lovely home. Many people helped with the removal and one church member even bought Gwen a fridge, the first she had ever owned. Once the family was settled in, church members were invited to see the house they had so thoughtfully provided and decorated. All were delighted with the result of their efforts.

On arriving at the front door of the house it was immediately obvious that the garden, too, needed considerable attention. Gwen soon came into her own, working hard on the small patch of ground at the front of the house and in the yard at the back. Before long, she had shrubs, perennials, roses and grass in the front garden. The back yard became a haven of tranquillity in a busy part of Glasgow as she used her gardening skills to transform the bare earth into a lush little garden with even a small garden pond.

However, it was not long before the reality of living in a big city was brought home to the family. It happened on a Sunday evening, about three weeks after the removal, when Donald and Gwen returned home from church. As Donald parked and locked the car, Gwen opened the front door, only to see a young man running down the stairs with Ruth's guitar on his shoulder and Donald's typewriter sitting on the top step of the staircase. Gwen had become used to workmen and church members helping to refurbish the house, so she was at first unsure whether this was a young person from the church whom she had not previously met. She therefore called to Donald who quickly came to the door and shouted,

"Who are you?"

The young man then began to retreat to the kitchen, the way he had come into the house, holding something like a knife in his hand. He wrenched the back door off its hinges, ran into the garden and jumped over the garden wall. Donald ran after him, but could not keep up with him. The police were called and it soon became clear that the young man had been in the house for some time: apart from stealing a good number of personal items, he had made himself a cup of tea and enjoyed some of Gwen's baking, including a luscious chocolate cake. The teapot was still warm!

As a result of the break-in, the house was fitted with security locks on doors and windows. During the years in Glasgow there was one further, unsuccessful, attempt to break into the house when a back window was pushed open as far as the security locks would allow and ornaments on the window ledge were pulled out into the garden. This happened when Donald was away from home but, fortunately, one of the ladies from the church had come home with Gwen that evening for a cup of tea. Gwen therefore did not have to cope with the situation on her own. It was unsettling to know that once again someone had tried to break in but also reassuring to know that the security systems had been effective.

For some time before Donald's arrival, church members had been holding a Late Night Outreach on a Friday evening which Donald liked to call 'Mission at Midnight'. For this outreach, the church halls were opened on alternate Fridays from 10pm until the early hours of the morning. Church members, who were not all young, went out onto the streets to talk to people and invite them in for a cup of tea or coffee and some biscuits.

Soon there was a constant flow of people coming in and out of the halls. Donald enthusiastically joined in with this outreach, as a participant, not as the leader. Not only did he invite people from the streets of Glasgow, but he joined others in going into the dance halls to extend the invitation to come to the Adelaide Place halls once the dance was over. Writing about these evenings in the Scottish Baptist Magazine of April 1971, Donald remarked,

"One never knows quite what an evening will bring forth and we have learned to go out in dependence on God and to trust the Holy Spirit to give us the words to say."

The church's own music group 'The Soul Seekers' played throughout each evening. At some point on some evenings there would be a short talk about the Christian faith, but most of the talking was done around tables as interested people chatted over tea or coffee. These were exciting evenings, but also very scary for those involved, as anything could happen.

One evening two young lads came in, a fifteen year old who was too drunk to stand and his sixteen year old friend who was trying to look after him. Concerned for their safety, and hating what alcohol did to young people, Donald took them home to their hostel where the sixteen year old said he would get them both into the hostel by using the fire escape! Donald was particularly moved when the fifteen year old, before he was totally incapable of speech, said to him,

"Youse folks are great . . .you're the only folks in this city who don't want our money."

On another occasion there was a young man who was the worse for wear. When Donald volunteered to take him home, some other church members accompanied him. On arriving at the man's home, Donald tried to help him onto the settee and began to speak of Christ, even although the man was too drunk to take in what was being said. One of the men with Donald, John Stewart, was astounded, quite sure that the man was not capable of listening to what was being said. Donald was on his knees beside the man, in a position of serving, speaking of the gospel, a spontaneous act which spoke so much about him.

It was not long before Donald had a clear view of the different challenges faced by the congregation in Adelaide Place. He detected five different worlds around the church, all isolated from each other. However, instead of focusing on their isolation, he regarded them as five different mission opportunities: the large numbers of people who flooded into the city centre at weekends to take advantage of the entertainment, the business community which was in the city during the week, the students who were staying in flats and residences close to the city centre, the community of people living around the church and the homeless who slept on the streets of the city each night.

Donald's heart was full of compassion for all these people and he longed to reach out to them with the gospel, but he also looked at the Adelaide Place church building and saw that it was no longer fit for purpose. He was convinced that the church would have to renovate their building as a statement of intent: a building which looked clean on the outside and was warm and welcoming inside would speak of a church which meant to stay in the city centre and minister to the needs of all who passed by. In spite of nervousness at the size of the task, church members responded enthusiastically to Donald's vision and quickly began raising the £6,000 to allow the facelift of the building to begin. Much more, however, was needed to complete the renovation of the building, so various trusts were approached and an appeal was made to other congregations in the Baptist Union of Scotland. Many people gave sacrificially and it was not long before the outside of the church was stone-cleaned. Passers-by began to notice the newly cleaned building and remark upon it, just what Donald had wanted!

Money came in from many different sources. One morning, Donald heard the post drop through the letterbox. He came out of his study and ran downstairs to pick up the letters. As he did so, he noticed that one envelope was quite bulky. On opening it, five hundred pounds fell out – an anonymous gift for the renovation of Adelaide Place! This was only one of a number of anonymous gifts, adding to the giving of church members and money obtained from a variety of other sources. All these gifts were a great encouragement to the church members as they took the risk of doing something radically different.

While the church building was being stone-cleaned and renovated, the work of the church went on as usual. Donald was particularly worried about the homeless youngsters in the city centre, many of whom came to the church halls as part of the 'Mission at Midnight'. Others simply came into the church when meetings were on, looking for somewhere warm and dry for a couple of hours. A young couple who were members of the church, Dr. Donald McLarty and his wife Dorothy, took some of these youngsters home from time to time, but Donald was convinced that a regular refuge was needed – a place where these youngsters could be safe.

One evening a young girl arrived at the church looking for somewhere to stay, but when Donald tried to find somewhere for her, he realised that there was nowhere for younger girls to go in Glasgow because lodging houses took older women only. Donald was horrified that a young woman could have nowhere to stay in Glasgow city centre, so he discussed the idea of a refuge for homeless youngsters with the church's deacons and then at a business meeting for the whole church; discussions were positive and, as a result, a decision was made to approach Glasgow District Council and inquire about renting a flat where homeless girls could be accommodated. Although there were also homeless young men in the city centre it was decided to have a flat for girls because they were so vulnerable when out on the city streets alone. The flat, in Buccleuch Street in the Garnethill area of the city centre, was named 'Elpis', meaning 'House of Hope', making clear that it was to be a place where homeless girls would find hope, love and care.

This was simply the beginning, for much had to be done before the flat was in a suitable condition to be opened as a refuge. First of all, there was a good deal of bureaucracy, which Donald found very irritating, but it had to be done if the project was to go ahead. Also, the flat was not in good order, so church members – particularly, but not exclusively, the young people of the church - set about renovating, cleaning and decorating it to make it comfortable for the first residents. It was a difficult job which needed the good organisation of

Duncan Dougall and his willing helpers to ensure all the tasks were completed, but eventually the flat was opened for business with two nurses looking after the girls, one engaged full time by the church and the other working part-time as a nurse and part-time in the flat.

Over the next few years 'Elpis' was so well used that it eventually outgrew the flat in Buccleuch Street and moved to Anderston where several flats could be combined into one hostel. Later it moved again, becoming part of the social work in Glasgow rather than simply a church based organisation but still holding to the original vision of caring for vulnerable young women.

Donald's practical concern for others was always obvious. One evening when he was in Glasgow's Central Station after a meeting with some other ministers, he noticed a man begging. While his companions went off for their trains, Donald went back to the man and worked hard to help him until 3am the next morning when finally some accommodation was found. On this occasion, not only did Donald spend hours finding the man accommodation, he also paid for it because the man had no money of his own.

Both Donald and Gwen gave of themselves unstintingly for others, often having people staying in the manse for long or short periods – just however long it took to help the person concerned. Some spent a few hours in the manse, receiving the immediate help they needed. A few were students who simply appreciated a home-from-home during term-time and were happy to be part of the family for a while. Many more, however, had been living on the streets of Glasgow or were in trouble of some kind and needed assistance to improve their circumstances.

One man whom Donald knew was an alcoholic who had been sober for a few months. He had the chance of going into a Church of Scotland hostel but had no money and felt that the clothes he owned were not good enough to wear at the interview for a place in the hostel. Also, after living on the streets, he smelled badly. Donald brought him to the manse, told him to have a bath and then called to Peter, who was in the house at the time,

"What is your neck size?"

It was not long before Peter found out why he had been asked such a strange question: the man came downstairs after his bath wearing Peter's shirt, tie and jacket as well as Donald's new cord shoes, socks and trousers! In addition, he had shaved off his beard, looked years younger and he no longer smelled. Clean and kitted out for the interview, he was accepted for a place in the hostel.

Another man regularly slept at the back of garages in a lane behind the manse. Donald often went out to check how he was doing and tried to find him a place to stay. However, there was a period of several months during the first winter when the man was not around and Donald became rather worried about him, until one morning there was a knock at the door. When Donald answered, there was the man standing on the doorstep saying,

"Just to tell you, meenister. I've been on holiday."

In fact, the man had been in jail. He always did something to make sure that he was arrested in the autumn and did not have to spend the winter outside.

Donald's ability to help people in distress was soon well known among Scottish churches. One evening, a medical student who attended Charlotte Baptist Chapel in Edinburgh unfortunately missed the last train home after spending the day in Glasgow. Before long, he met a young man who kindly offered him some accommodation for the night, but was horrified when the accommodation turned out to be an abandoned car at the back of Buchanan Street bus station. Being a medical student he quickly realised that the lad had trouble with his breathing and needed urgent medical attention, so he took him to hospital where drugs were given and the young man began to feel better. The medical student then contacted Donald, who alerted the social services to the lad's need of accommodation, particularly urgent because of his health problems. He was told that accommodation could be provided, so sent the lad to the social work department. Peter, who had been on nightshift on the buses, arrived home and met the young man before he left the manse. He was therefore astonished to see the same young man crossing the road in front of his bus at 2.30am the next morning. When Peter told Donald what he had seen, he was very angry that his previous day's arrangements had fallen through and contacted the social work department as soon as it was open for business at 9am. Unfortunately, the lad was never seen again and so Donald did not find out what had happened to him.

Hospitality was extended to all who needed help. One day someone from another church contacted Donald to ask about accommodation in Glasgow for a prisoner on weekend release. The man had been in prison for murder and was in training for freedom. He had weekend release coming up, but nowhere to go. Donald and Gwen offered to look after him, so he stayed in the manse for the weekend.

A number of vulnerable girls also stayed at the manse, sometimes for long periods. They became very fond of Donald and Gwen, regarding them as substitute parents and even calling them 'Mops and Pops'. Some of these girls had foster parents with whom Donald was in regular touch; he felt he learned a lot from them about how the social work system worked, while the girls themselves opened Donald's eyes as to how their world worked. However, these girls also knew that Donald had high standards: he expected them to behave themselves, particularly while they were staying at the manse. One day, Peter returned home from a shift on the buses to find one of the girls on the doorstep. Being slightly drunk, she knew Donald would be angry about her behaviour and so had waited until Peter came home to let her in. As Peter approached she said, "I've been to the pub. Pops'll kill me!"

Peter let her in and made sure that she went to her bedroom.

Donald even went out onto the streets to rescue these girls if necessary, taking Peter with him if he was going to a place where a man should not be on his own. The police knew that Donald was always willing to help people in distress and sometimes phoned to tell him about youngsters known to Donald who were in trouble. One night they phoned at 3am to say that one of the girls had been found walking on a motorway and when picked up by the police she had mentioned Donald's name. Donald immediately went to the police station and brought her home to the manse.

Donald's compassion for others was a constant theme in the deacons' meetings at Adelaide Place. He was not the best organiser of business and often these meetings would go on late into the night as Donald's passion to help others overtook all consideration of time. As the years went on, this passion grew and Donald was constantly coming up with new ideas for reaching out in the centre of the city. The deacons found it hard to deal with all these new ideas, but they recognised that at the heart of all the ideas was a passion to help others in Christ's name.

The social side of compassion was, indeed, only one part of Donald's ministry in Adelaide Place. Early on in his ministry he encouraged young men in their twenties to take responsibility within the church and become part of the deacons' court; he had an ability to trust young people and was willing to take a risk in appointing them to positions which, in the past, had been occupied by much older men. The youth fellowship, which had grown and matured under the previous minister, was ready to move on and Donald gave them the opportunity to do so within Adelaide Place. This was the beginning of young men becoming really useful in the work of the church.

Donald's preaching abilities soon became well known and a number of students, many from overseas, began to attend the church. Because of his great gift for preaching several young men, both those who grew up in Adelaide Place and those who came for a short time as students, became preachers themselves, many more than might have been expected from a small city centre congregation. The young people of the church had such a high regard for Donald and for his preaching that each

Wednesday they would go straight to church at the end of their working day, eat sandwiches for their tea, attend the regular church choir practice and then, without exception, go to the church prayer meeting where Donald would preach in addition to the time given over to prayer. They particularly appreciated Donald's ability to clearly explain the teaching of the Bible.

Complementing Donald's encouragement to young men in the church, Gwen's concern was for the young women. She started a regular meeting in the manse for these women and also introduced them to the Women's Auxiliary where they would meet women of all ages. As a result, the women of the church came alive under her care, becoming a flourishing part of the church's ministry. The ladies particularly appreciated her friendliness, her care for others and her baking!

It was not only the young people who were encouraged to play a greater part in the work of the church. In September 1972 Donald wrote a letter to all members and friends of Adelaide Place in which he outlined his plans to give every member a real opportunity to influence the decision-making process of the church. The church meeting had already approved in principal his plan to set up six 'Commissions', but now he explained the commissions in detail and asked members to serve on a commission of their choice. These Commissions were Mission and Evangelism, Worship and Fellowship, Overseas Missions, Work among Children and Youth, Social Responsibility and, finally, Care and Maintenance of the Church Building. Donald envisaged the commissions meeting at least three times each year to consider their specific area of responsibility and then to bring recommendations to the deacons' court and the church as a whole. In the letter Donald wrote,

"The benefits of such a scheme will be clear. The deacons and the minister will be stimulated by a constant stream of constructive criticism and fresh prayer-inspired thinking and every member will know and feel himself to be an active and responsible member of the Body of Christ. We shall be helped to be what we ought to be – <u>workers together with God.</u>"

Not all the commissions were successfully implemented, but some of them became very helpful parts of the church's ministry for many years afterwards.

Another, very significant, part of Donald's ministry began with an invitation to speak at the Chinese Fellowship in Glasgow. Before long, he was speaking regularly at their meetings on a Sunday afternoon and had built up good friendships with the leaders of the group. When Donald found out that the building in which they were meeting was due for demolition he said,

"Come to us",

and so began a productive relationship between the Adelaide Place congregation and the Glasgow Chinese Christian Fellowship. They began by using the small hall for their meetings but soon had to use the large hall to accommodate the numbers attending.

A number of Chinese began to attend the regular church services in Adelaide Place as well as their own Fellowship on a Sunday afternoon, with the result that it was not long before some of them were baptised and joined the church. Indeed they soon became very active members with some taking leadership roles within the church, alongside an excellent developing relationship between the Adelaide Place congregation and members of the Glasgow Chinese Christian Fellowship. A demonstration of this relationship was clearly shown in the November 1979 edition of the Scottish Baptist Magazine which included a photograph of Donald and the pastor of the Chinese Fellowship, Chi Khen Pan, sharing a baptismal service. Donald was particularly pleased at the warmth of the relationship, remarking,

"As a young man I wanted to go to China as a missionary but was unable to do so. Now the Chinese are coming to Glasgow and I am sharing fellowship with them!"

Before long, there was another group using the church premises – the newly formed African and Caribbean Fellowship. They, too, enjoyed a close relationship with the Adelaide Place congregation and with Donald. The church was beginning to attract people from many different nations and Donald was particularly pleased, especially when these people played an active part in church life. He wrote an article for the June 1980 edition of the Scottish Baptist Magazine entitled "Twenty-five nations represented at service." The article was a report of a very special Sunday when morning worship had been led by a Chinese, the preacher for that service coming from Kowloon in Vietnam, and the evening service had been led by the newly formed African and Caribbean Fellowship. At the morning service 19 nations had been represented, but by the end of the evening service twenty-five nations in total had been represented in Adelaide Place that day. Donald was ecstatic and wrote,

"What a witness to the power of the gospel to make men one! What better proof that Jesus Christ is the Hope, the Only Hope of our divided world."

Apart from the two services, there was a meal in the afternoon. Again, Donald rejoiced in the unity experienced when people from many nations ate together and then shared in a communion service.

"At the end of the meal, and as we sat together at table, we shared together in the Lord's Supper. That was a sacred moment, in which heaven itself came down to meet us."

As all the different ministries of the church began to grow, it became apparent that Donald could not cope with all the work on his own. When the deacons considered whom they might appoint to share the responsibilities with Donald, they began to consider Paul Gardner who was studying at the Bible Training Institute in Glasgow. He and his wife had joined the church near the start of their studies in 1971 and then Paul became a deacon before later on becoming an elder in the church. Paul and his wife had wanted to go to Thailand as missionaries, but their plans had fallen through. Although naturally disappointed that these plans had come to nothing, the deacons considered that Paul was now eminently suitable for the post which was about to be created. Paul was asked to consider the pastoral ministry and when he agreed to do this the process of accreditation with the Baptist Union of Scotland began. This process took approximately a year, but by the end of the year the Union had agreed to become a partner with the church, appointing Paul as Pioneer Minister for Glasgow City Centre, based at Adelaide Place and under Donald's leadership. For the next four years he worked alongside Donald, developing a variety of ministries. Paul took an active part in all aspects of church life, such as the Monday night meetings when they both helped at a meeting for alcoholics, run by Miss Irene Allan and her team. Other members of Adelaide Place also helped out, one of whom was Bill Dougall. He recalls:

"At the meetings the people there were given a hot drink and something to eat; then there were the hymns. If the hymn book was opened it would be at one of the favourites, the bottom of the page black with the hands which had held it over the years. Then Donald would give his talk and I'm sure his words would be remembered by all those who were present."

Paul also pioneered children's work in schools around Glasgow city centre while his wife, Alice, started a Girls' Brigade. In addition, he began meetings in three old people's homes and in a community centre near the STV studios. Paul thoroughly enjoyed his years working with Donald, developing a good working relationship. He saw Donald as

"a true pioneer in many ways, a man of vision, integrity and humour. Above all he was a humble man who boasted only "in the cross". He lived and breathed the Gospel and was never happier than when seeing men and women surrendering to Christ. As a pastor he was very approachable and full of wise counsel."

He particularly appreciated Donald's preaching: his ability to explain God's word in a practical way and his use of varied and down-to-earth illustrations in his sermons, especially his ability to use poetry effectively.

Paul also appreciated Donald's sense of justice and his anger at injustice. On one occasion, however, Donald's quick reaction to a perceived injustice almost had them arrested! Paul and Donald were on their way back from a pastoral visit when Donald noticed two men under a bridge being beaten by two other men wielding batons. Donald wasted no time in enlisting Paul's help to disarm the attackers. Their intervention was successful, but only then did they learn that the two 'victims' were in fact in the process of being arrested by plain clothes police! Fortunately, Paul had held on to the two men, who were then handed over to the police. However, the two policemen were very angry, even suggesting that Donald's action could have led to his arrest and imprisonment if the arrest had been prevented. Donald, too, was angry, pointing out that too much violence had been used and he would not hesitate to report the policemen to their superiors. Providentially for Donald and Paul all ended well, but Paul experienced Donald's intense sense of justice which could, at times, lead to hasty and not always the wisest course of action.

In all his previous churches, Donald had always been happy to work with people of all denominations to preach the gospel, so he was pleased to help start lunchtime services in the Renfield Street Centre which was close to Adelaide Place. He also welcomed the arrival of Arthur Blessitt who was walking around much of Europe carrying a large cross, arranging with George Duncan of the Tron Church of Scotland to have Arthur Blessitt preach at a morning service in the Tron and at an evening service in Adelaide Place. Before the service Arthur Blessitt, his wife and his four children, whose names all began with J, came to the manse for tea. The youngest was so tired that he fell sound asleep and did not eat his tea! That evening the church was full to capacity, with queues right round the church as people tried to get in for the service. Some even sat on the window ledges because there was so little room left and Arthur Blessitt even had to step around people to reach the pulpit. It was a wonderful occasion, with enthusiastic worship and preaching, an evening never to be forgotten!

The next morning, however, would be remembered for very different reasons: dry rot was discovered on a main beam which held up the church sanctuary. Experts were called in and it soon became clear that there was extensive, previously unnoticed, dry rot in the building, so the church was faced with more expense. Then at the end of a morning service a few weeks later there was a terrific noise when some of the ceiling and a number of the window ledges came down. The next day Rev. Peter Barber, one of Donald's close friends, heard about the incident and phoned Donald. Always enjoying humour he said,

"I hear you preached so well, Donald, that the ceiling came down!"

All were relieved, nevertheless, that the service with Arthur Blessitt where so many people had been crammed into the building had gone ahead safely and they thanked God for protection from danger.

In the midst of all this activity connected to Adelaide Place, Donald was also playing a part in the Baptist Union of Scotland. He was not as involved as he had been during his years in Stirling, but he continued to serve on committees and take an active interest in the affairs of the Union. A man of principle, he was not afraid to stand up for what he believed to be right, even when most people disagreed with him, on one occasion resigning from a committee and on another occasion standing up at a Baptist Union Assembly to make his views passionately clear.

The frantic pace of life eventually took its toll. Gwen, as always, looked after him lovingly, making sure that his diabetes remained stable, but there were several occasions when he had bad 'hypos' because a meeting ran late or someone needed his attention and he consequently was unable to have a meal at the correct time. By 1976 the pace of life had become so much that he had a heart attack and was forced to rest and recuperate. Gwen made full use of her nursing skills, looking after him at home, but nevertheless he had to take several months off work. Paul Gardner took over much of Donald's role during these months while church members, particularly the elders and deacons, shouldered extra responsibilities until Donald was well enough to return to work full time.

Over the next few years until his retirement Donald continued his accustomed pace of work but by the end of a day would often be at the end of his physical ability. His urge to preach the gospel was as strong as ever and he pushed himself to the limit, wanting to move on at a pace others sometimes found difficult to handle. Nonetheless, even when unwell he was considering others. One Sunday morning one of the deacons, John Stewart, realised that Donald hardly had the strength to finish his sermon. As soon as Donald finished preaching, John took him through to the vestry, managed to get him to lie down on the floor and phoned for an ambulance. Before the ambulance arrived a man came in to speak to Donald, wanting some help. In spite of being unwell and having to lie on the floor, Donald spoke to the man, giving him the help he needed.

There was no doubt that Donald thoroughly enjoyed the challenges of working in Glasgow, but he also yearned to travel. It was while looking for financial support for Adelaide Place that his dream of travelling to the USA became a reality through the Baptist Heritage Program, based in Washington D.C. A number of Scottish Baptist ministers had been to churches in the USA with the help of this program, including one of Donald's friends, Bill Porch. He put Donald in touch with a representative of the Program who suggested that several American churches might be able to support Adelaide Place by providing finance. In addition to finance, a speaking tour was arranged so that Donald could explain the challenges faced by the members of Adelaide Place.

Consequently, in October 1979 he and Gwen were able to fly out to New York before continuing on to their first church visit - the First Baptist Church in San Antonio, Texas. They enjoyed fellowship at church services but were also taken to see some of the tourist attractions, including The Alamo. Donald bought a cowboy hat and enjoyed posing for a photograph while wearing the hat!

From Texas they moved on to Greensboro, North Carolina, where Donald preached at an evening service and at a mid-week prayer service as well as speaking to a group of pastors. Donald and Gwen were also guests at a Stewardship Dinner. Their names appeared in the church's weekly leaflet, with Donald described as Dr. Donald McCallum, an honour which amused him greatly as he had never had the opportunity to gain any kind of degree! However, their main memory of the visit was the kindness of the church members who welcomed them into their church fellowship and also took them sightseeing in the Blue Ridge Mountains.

The third church visited was the First Baptist Church in Knoxville, Tennessee, where Donald preached at two morning services. Once again the church members were extremely kind and welcoming on the Sunday, describing them in the church leaflet as "a distinguished couple" and also taking them to visit Great Smoky Mountains National Park later on in the week.

After speaking at three churches, Donald and Gwen ended their tour of the USA with a visit to friends in Virginia. These friends who had known Donald since the early days in Stenhouse, Edinburgh, gave them a wonderful holiday, taking them to Skyline Drive and Shenandoah National Park in Virginia as well as the White House. An unforgettable USA trip ended with a final meeting with some Baptists in New York before flying home to Glasgow.

A second opportunity to travel came in the spring of 1981. For some years a number of African students had been attending Adelaide Place, with some of them such as Segun Komolafe taking a leadership role within the church during their years in Glasgow. Early in 1981 Segun asked Donald and Gwen to pay a pastoral visit to Nigeria so that they could visit the ex-Glasgow Nigerians and their families. Needless to say, Donald and Gwen were delighted to accept the invitation. Donald wrote two articles about their experiences in the September and October editions of Scottish Baptist Magazine, noting that

"We did not go as tourists to see the country, although, in fact, we saw a great deal of it, but to visit our people and their families, to encourage them in the Lord and to be ourselves refreshed by their fellowship. We received such

love as will make the experience one of the most memorable of our lives."

On landing in Nigeria, first of all they were taken to Kaduna where they visited the Baptist Pastors College and Donald had the unique experience on the Sunday morning of preaching through an interpreter to a Yaruba-speaking congregation in the Evangelical Church of West Africa. Later on that day he preached to an English-speaking Baptist congregation. The morning service

"began with a great shout of joy from a man who seemed to leap out of the front pews. As he raised his voice, an exultant procession entered the door and proceeded up one aisle, across the front of the church and down the other aisle, complete with donkey (2 men under a sheet) and rider and shouting people. It was Palm Sunday all right! I felt transported across the centuries to the first Palm Sunday of long ago."

From Kaduna Donald and Gwen flew to Lagos to stay with Segun Komolafe and his family. They were met at the airport by Segun who had travelled hundreds of miles in the previous weeks and months in order to arrange their programme and hospitality. He took them to Ife where he and his wife and family lived. While there, Donald thoroughly enjoyed preaching to large congregations in their church at two morning services, then later that same day he preached at an Anglican church in the city. He particularly appreciated sharing in the Easter Communion service.

From Ife they moved on to Ibadan to meet a number of ex-Glasgow families. Their accommodation was in a Christian conference centre where they enjoyed meeting Christians from a number of nations and denominations.

Donald preached in the Orita Mefa Baptist Church adjacent to the University where he was particularly appreciative of the warm, welcoming atmosphere.

The Nigerian adventure ended in Kaduna where Donald and Gwen were able to rest for a couple of days before being driven to Kano to catch the plane home. Always friendly, Donald spent some time chatting to a young man in the foyer of their hotel. The man had been to university in Yugoslavia where he had encountered Marxism and he was happy to talk to Donald about his struggle to reconcile his Marxism with his Muslim faith and to listen as Donald took the opportunity to share his own faith.

Once back in Glasgow, Donald and Gwen were just as busy as ever. The church was growing steadily with many different nationalities attending, a number of students making the church their spiritual home while in Glasgow, frequent baptismal services where people openly confessed their faith in Christ and a good core of members who were willing to give of themselves to see the gospel preached in Glasgow city centre. Nevertheless, both Donald and Gwen felt that it was time for them to retire. Donald would be sixty-five in February 1982 so he informed the church deacons that he intended to retire in the June of that year. At Donald's final baptismal service in Adelaide Place on 16th May 1982 sixteen people were baptised, confessing their faith in Christ Jesus.

After living in a tied manse all their married lives, Donald and Gwen had to begin looking for somewhere to live during their retirement. As they still had many contacts in the Stirling area, including Donald's sister and brother-in-law Ruby and Willie Dudgeon, they decided to look for a house to rent in that area. However, it was not long before a friend in Kippen, Penny Coles, made them a very generous offer of a small cottage. At that time Penny was living in a cottage which had originally been two separate dwellings. She offered to divide the cottage again, giving them half. They would need to completely renovate their half to make it habitable but the offer was an incredibly generous one, allowing them to become home owners for the first time in their lives.

Donald and Gwen were overwhelmed by the offer but saw it as God's provision for their retirement. Over the next year much had to be done to secure grants and make sure that work on the cottage went ahead. As the work proceeded well and the cottage began to take shape Donald and Gwen began to look forward to retirement in the lovely village of Kippen, only ten miles from Stirling which they knew so well.

Adelaide Place church arranged a farewell evening. It was a very happy occasion with many friends attending – a real celebration of Donald's years of ministry in the church. During Donald's years in Glasgow Adelaide Place had grown, developing a variety of ministries and expanding its horizons to include many different nationalities. Donald and Gwen were ready to move on and the church too had to look to the future.

There had been big changes in family life during the years in Glasgow. Donald conducted Ruth's wedding in 1975 when she married Charles Millican and by the time of Donald's retiral there were three grand-children – Donald, Kirsty and Calum. In addition, over a few of these years Peter was working away from home in Liverpool and Birmingham.

It was time for a new beginning. No-one could imagine Donald actually settling down to a quiet life in retiral, but both Donald and Gwen looked forward to a slightly slower pace of life in the lovely village of Kippen. Nevertheless, Donald's enthusiasm for preaching the gospel was undiminished. In the April 1982 edition of The Scottish Baptist magazine he wrote

"It is a great time to be alive – because Jesus is alive! What excited the disciples in Acts and should excite us, is not simply the miracle of the resurrection, and that is exciting enough, but its meaning. It gives us Good News to share . . . . It gives us a Fellowship to which to belong . . . . It gives us a Companion on our way . . .And it gives us a whole new dimension to our lives, a dimension of eternity."

Chapter 10:

Retiral – new opportunities

It was July 1982 when Donald and Gwen moved into their newly-renovated cottage in Kippen. The move from the large house in Glasgow to a small cottage meant that a lot of their furniture was not suitable and, worst of all for Donald, there was not enough storage space for all his books! Eventually, he did have to leave some books behind in Glasgow but he still managed to retain a very large number for his new study in Kippen. Gwen was kept busy, sorting out furniture and other household items that could be used in Kippen before disposing of the remainder. This was a long task, but the thought of the lovely cottage in Kippen spurred her on. "Think small!" she kept saying as she furnished the cottage and made it into a lovely, welcoming home.

Donald's brother-in-law, Willie Dudgeon, did a great deal of work in the cottage, making the kitchen habitable, putting in stairs up to the loft in order to create a bedroom and building shelving for Donald's many books. Gwen happily set about creating a lovely garden once more, even to the extent of bringing the pond from the Glasgow garden. The family cat definitely appreciated the move! In spite of being a Glasgow cat, on her first day in Kippen she ran out into the garden and settled down in the sun, making clear her intention to enjoy the lovely surroundings of her new home!

Once again both house and garden were soon flourishing under Gwen's care and it was not long before both Donald and Gwen were feeling very much at home in Kippen. They decided to give their little cottage a name – Tigh na Sigh – Gaelic for 'House of Peace'. Over the next few years they would enjoy the peace of their cottage and village but, typically, they did not keep this peace to themselves. Needless to say, many visitors were soon enjoying hospitality in 'Tigh na Sigh', appreciating the lovely little cottage and its garden, as well as the welcome given by Donald and Gwen.

Gwen understood perfectly that Donald did not know the meaning of the word 'retiral', so it was no surprise to hear very quickly that he had been asked to preach in Stirling Baptist Church while the minister, Rev. James Taylor, was on sabbatical. Donald relished the task, delighting in the opportunity to preach in Stirling, especially since he and Gwen had once again become members of the church.

With his passion for the gospel as great as ever, Donald thoroughly enjoyed returning to preach each Sunday in the church where he had ministered for so many years and was grateful when told of lives touched by God during this time. One couple whom Donald knew very well told him his sermons had challenged them to attend church more regularly. Some people from outside the

Stirling area came occasionally to services in Stirling and they, too, were helped. One of these was a man who came to an evening service feeling down in spirits and hoping to receive some encouragement. He left feeling so uplifted that many years later he could still remember practically every word that was preached.

Donald and Gwen thoroughly enjoyed being back in Stirling Baptist Church where they still had so many friends, and soon they were making many new friends too. Preaching in Stirling brought back happy memories, but it was not long before Donald was involved in something completely new to him. A few months after moving to Kippen, he was approached by Dr Harold Lyon of Strathcarron Hospice, asking if he would be willing to become their chaplain. Dr Lyon was a member of Stirling Baptist Church and the founder of the hospice. When working as a geriatrician in Falkirk Royal Infirmary he had become interested in the hospice movement and was determined to see one established in central Scotland. After a great deal of work by many people, Strathcarron Hospice had opened in April 1981, with the administrator doubling as the chaplain. The growth of the hospice meant, however, that a full-time chaplain was now required. Donald thought carefully before accepting the offer of the post of chaplain, making clear that if the Baptist Union of Scotland ever asked him to do anything for them then he would need to relinquish the hospice post.

Working in the hospice was a learning experience for Donald. His main objective was to be with the patients and with the staff if they needed him, so he went round the wards every day, getting to know the patients and their families very quickly. He also spent time with day care patients, sitting among them as they chatted to each other, happy to join in the conversation. They, in turn, appreciated his keen sense of humour and his fount of stories. He spent hours with people, reminiscing about the war, listening while people said what they wanted to say, giving of his time as if he had all the time in the world. All the patients and their families knew that any confidences would be kept: they could trust him completely.

Strathcarron Hospice wanted to look after the families of their patients too and Donald was good at dealing with families, talking with them for many hours, a very comforting presence but also very straightforward, not glossing over the facts. All involved in the hospice appreciated Donald's gentleness and care, none more so than the patients in the wards. One patient was completely convinced that Donald was a doctor because he came round the wards so frequently. One morning he said to Donald,

"It is so good that you come round the wards every day. If you hadn't become a doctor you would have made a good minister!"

Apart from talking to patients and their families, Donald also took part in some of the extra activities arranged by the hospice, such as firework parties, Christmas parties and summer fetes. He joined in with all of these, often bringing Gwen along too. Princess Anne became the hospice's friend, visiting regularly and Donald was introduced to her on several occasions.

Molly Parsons, the matron of the hospice, greatly appreciated the contribution made by Donald during his time there, particularly because "he was so humble and quiet. I had never met a man of God like him." The hospice staff all realised that he wanted to spend time with people, not caring about time himself. Fortunately they also understood his diabetes, so when he had become so absorbed in ministering to a patient or a relative that he had not noticed it was time for a meal they gently took him off to lunch.

Donald loved his time at the hospice, where he was continually learning new things. In good weather he enjoyed the beautiful drive from Kippen to Denny, where the hospice was located, often taking the minor road across the moors so that he could better appreciate the countryside. On most Sundays during this time he was also preaching at churches throughout Scotland. Donald and Gwen covered huge mileages in their car at weekends, enjoying the experience of seeing many churches, but when the Baptist Union of Scotland asked him to help the Baptist Church in Wigtown, in the south-west of Scotland, Donald knew that it was time to relinquish his post at the hospice and move on to a different challenge.

At that time, the Baptist Church in Wigtown was relatively new and was supported by the Southern Baptists in the USA. They had sent a young couple, Bob and Marsha Ford, who had been in Wigtown for two years. Their ministry was greatly appreciated, with the church growing steadily, but they were due to go back to the States for six months. Bob Ford contacted the Baptist Union of Scotland and asked if there was any retired minister who could look after the church and live in the manse for six or seven months. Rev. Peter Barber, who was then Secretary of the Baptist Union of Scotland, recommended Donald.

The Fords invited Donald and Gwen to stay with them for a few days so that they could meet people and decide whether or not they should take up the Baptist Union's suggestion. They accepted the Ford's offer of a short visit and went to Wigtown, spending time with church members and learning about the church as well as discussing the matter at length. It was a big decision to make, because it meant leaving the cottage in Kippen for several months and moving away from family in the central belt of Scotland. After a few days of meetings and discussion, Bob Ford asked if they would consider coming to Wigtown. Sitting in the lounge of the Wigtown manse Donald looked across at Gwen and said,

"What do you think, Gwen?"

but she quickly replied, "Donald, it is entirely your decision."

His immediate answer was,

"Yes, I would really like to come!"

Consequently, in the spring of 1986 Donald and Gwen moved temporarily into the church's large and beautiful manse, 'Applegarth', overlooking the Solway Firth. They were soon involved in all of the church's ministries – Sunday services in the County Buildings, Trail Blazers for children on Tuesday evenings, weekly prayer and Bible study meetings in the manse, monthly services in a local hospital and in a home for senior citizens, regular contact with an open prison in the area and also regular contact with a special needs school. Their lives were full, but they loved it!

Being very friendly, they soon knew many people in the

community. Donald made sure that the local newsagent ordered his favourite newspaper, The Guardian, while Gwen enjoyed going to the local shops where she would chat to the shopkeepers and other customers. They also appreciated living in the beautiful manse, where the vine growing in the conservatory was a constant source of interest. Needless to say, visitors to the manse were always made very welcome.

"I think that started Wigtown's love affair with Donald and Gwen and their love affair with Wigtown," remarked Donald King who was secretary of the church at the time. *"They became very popular in Wigtown with both our church people and non church people of the community. Wigtown is a small caring community and everyone just loved them. His ministry and witness were much appreciated by all."*

Donald's caring nature and his ability to speak to everyone, whatever their circumstances, were particularly appreciated. A number of people who went through difficult experiences at that time found him to be kind and understanding in their distress. They also were thankful for Gwen's support, a true helpmeet to Donald.

Church members were astonished at Donald's energy! As well as preaching and carrying out the duties expected of him, he regularly wrote to Members of Parliament about social and political issues. His social conscience was as strong as ever, so whenever there was a matter where he felt he could exert some Christian influence he wrote to the appropriate MP and encouraged his church members to do the same.

As well as taking part in all the church activities and meeting people, Donald and Gwen enjoyed exploring the district. Wigtownshire was completely new to them and they were charmed by its beauty and peace. Such was their enthusiasm for the area that family members were quick to visit them, filling up the large manse! Their 40th wedding anniversary on July 17th 1986 was a good excuse for a family gathering when all enjoyed a lovely weekend in 'Applegarth'. Church members and friends also joined in the celebrations, wishing Donald and Gwen much happiness and one church member, the local baker, donating a beautiful cake. As always, Donald was very appreciative of Gwen, without whom he could not have had such a fulfilling ministry.

When considering the temporary move to Wigtown, Gwen had been a little concerned about Donald's diabetes, wanting to be sure that he would have good care from medical staff in the area. She was assured that medical care was excellent and soon found it to be so. During the months in Wigtown there were one or two difficult moments when Donald needed to slow down a little, but on the whole he coped very well. One incident, though, was potentially more serious. It happened just after Donald had been for a walk to St Ninian's cave with some of the young people of the church.

Donald had taken the car with him and he began to drive home, expecting to be back in Wigtown before his next meal was due. However, the extra energy he had used up during the walk meant that he was soon experiencing a 'hypo' and he drove the car off the road into the edge of a small wood. Fortunately, a couple driving past saw his car go off the road and came to his rescue. They kindly took him back to 'Applegarth' where Gwen was soon able to give him sugar and a good meal. Ruth and Charles were visiting Wigtown at the time, so they were able to find the car and arrange for it to be brought back to Wigtown. The local police, who by then had heard of the incident, were concerned only for Donald's wellbeing. He had gone off the road at a point which was well known for minor accidents.

The six months in Wigtown sped past and it was time for Bob and Marsha Ford to return. However, this was not the end of Donald and Gwen's contact with Wigtown Baptist Church. Over the next few years they were invited back to take meetings on several occasions and also moved into 'Applegarth' again for a few months when the church was without a minister. They even spent the Christmas of 1988 in Wigtown, where some of the family joined them to celebrate the occasion in the beautiful surroundings of Wigtownshire. Charles and Ruth were particularly appreciative of the kindness of church members who left a very large soft toy in 'Applegarth' for the children – from Santa, of course!

The Wigtown Church had met regularly in the County Buildings for a number of years, but when these buildings were due for renovation church members began to look for alternative accommodation. Donald was on one of his visits to Wigtown when a building in the town – a former primary school - became available, so he and some of the church members went to see it. They stood outside on the grass to have a good look at the building, and then Donald led them in prayer.

"If God wants us to have this, He'll provide the money", Donald remarked.

The church did not actually ask anyone for money but, incredibly, over the course of a weekend people gave very generously and enough money was raised to purchase the building.

Donald and Gwen spent many happy months serving the Wigtown Church over the course of a number of years. Their first six months had introduced them to the people they had grown to love and they were always pleased to return. Once back in Kippen, however, there were other challenges to meet, other churches to which they could minister.

One of these churches was very close to home and close to Donald's heart: Cornton Baptist Church in Stirling. When the church's pastor left in 1990 to take up another post, Rev. Jim Taylor became the interim moderator, helping the church to find another minister, but the church also wanted an interim pastor so they invited Donald to take up this post. Despite being himself an interim moderator of another church at the time – Wester Hailes in Edinburgh – Donald gladly accepted Cornton's invitation. He was particularly delighted to be of service to Cornton because of his personal interest in the area: it was during his time as minister of Stirling Baptist Church that a Sunday school had been started there, and from this small beginning the church had been planted, becoming established as a separate fellowship in 1978.

Donald and Gwen were happy to be back in Cornton, renewing long-standing friendships as well as making new friends. All appreciated their contribution to church life, as the deacons of the church were happy to acknowledge in the following tribute:

"In accepting the invitation, Donald brought with him a lifetime of experience of ministry, a lifetime of commitment to the ministry, a wealth of wisdom, a spiritual well of great depth, a love of people and what proved, at times, to be a

healthy disregard for the sometimes protracted and painful processes of decision making of a congregational style of church government.

Donald McCallum loved people. He was a good choice for Cornton at that time and was able with his grace and patience to guide the church in their search for a new pastor. His preaching was a blessing to many and his pastoral gifts brought strength and comfort as required. He was able to make himself at home with people to the extent that he was accepted in some of the homes as much as a member of the family as a pastor.

Two things stand out in the memories of so many people in Cornton about Donald that they are worthy of mention. Donald was diabetic, carefully tended throughout his life by that extraordinary woman he had married, his wife Gwen. Always conscious of how he might have been health-wise without Gwen's loving care, when asked how he was, Donald invariably replied, "I'm far better than I have any right to be."

The other is that Donald knew that he had a call from God to preach. He was a minister of the Gospel and he was a pastor to the people wherever he ministered but his prime calling to which he remained true was as a preacher. He was ministered to by the Holy Spirit and inspired in his studies and preaching and not just the name of Donald McCallum but the MAN himself will long be remembered throughout Scotland and Cornton in particular."

All this time, Donald was also helping the Wester Hailes Church to find a minister. On some Sundays when he had to be in Edinburgh rather than Cornton he suggested to the Cornton deacons that they should have the assistant minister of Wester Hailes, Robert Young, to preach. It was no surprise to Donald that the Cornton members were so impressed by Robert that they asked him to be their next minister!

Once Cornton had their own minister again, Donald was soon preaching in a number of churches across Scotland. Some churches wanted a preacher for a single Sunday only, but others appreciated Donald's pastoral and preaching gifts over a longer period. Donald continued to serve the Wester Hailes church, preaching during a time of vacancy. He had also preached regularly in the church when their previous minister had been seriously ill, so the people there grew to know and love him. For a time he was also interim moderator of Alva Baptist Church, another church he knew well because of its proximity to Stirling. Kinmylies Baptist Church in Inverness also appreciated his ministry over an extended period when Donald and Gwen spent a number of long weekends in Inverness, getting to know and love the people and giving of themselves to the church there.

When the Baptist Church in Bearsden, near Glasgow, was going through a period of vacancy they asked Donald to preach for a couple of Sundays. On the second Sunday they approached him and asked if he could preach regularly during their vacancy because they were so delighted with his preaching: it was just what the church needed at that time when they did not have their own minister. Thus it came about that Donald and Gwen regularly drove from Kippen to Bearsden on a Sunday, enjoying the drive through beautiful countryside before spending the day with the church. Bearsden was not too far from Kippen, so they sometimes went home between the morning and evening services, while at other times appreciating the hospitality provided by church members.

Another church close to home, Denny Baptist Church, was also grateful for Donald's ministry. During the years of Donald's retirement the church twice experienced a vacancy. On each occasion Donald became the interim moderator, helping them to find a new minister, taking mid-week meetings, visiting people in their homes and preaching at Sunday services. They were very appreciative of his willingness to serve them, but worried that sometimes he was at the limit of his physical ability.

One evening when Donald had been chairing a deacons' meeting in Denny, Gwen became anxious at the lateness of the hour. Donald was not good at finishing such meetings on time, but this was particularly late and she became more and more worried about him, knowing that he should have been home for supper. Eventually she phoned the secretary of the church who told her that the meeting had finished some time before. Even more worried, Gwen phoned Peter and asked him to go looking for Donald.

Just before Peter set off, his wife Ann-Marie suggested that he should phone the police so that they could also look for Donald. Peter did this, delaying his departure by a few minutes. The delay was crucial, for in answer to prayer Peter very quickly saw Donald driving in front of him as he approached the large roundabout beside the Stirling motorway service station. Donald knew he was 'hypo' and stopped the car, but in the confusion caused by the 'hypo' he did not know where he was. The police, who arrived at the same time as Peter, drove Donald's car into the service station where it was left until the next morning. Peter, meanwhile, took Donald into the service station's cafe, bought him some food and then drove him home. The next morning Donald was his usual bright self, but Gwen and Peter were exhausted after their efforts to secure Donald's safety!

This experience was not, however, the only time when Donald was miraculously protected from harm. One other occasion stands out, showing how wonderfully God looked after him. When Billy Graham came to Glasgow in June 1991, Stirling Baptist Church hired a bus to take a number of people to one of the meetings. Donald was one of these people but, unfortunately, Gwen was unable to join him because she was in Birmingham visiting her brother who was seriously ill at the time.

On the day, Donald had an early tea and, before joining the others on the bus, went to visit his sister who was in hospital in Stirling. After thoroughly enjoying the meeting in Glasgow he began to make his way through the large crowds back to his bus, but he soon became separated from the other members of his party. It had been several hours since his tea and he was now beginning to need another meal.

Ruth had also been at the meeting, singing in the choir. As she, too, made her way through the large crowd, out of the corner of her eye she noticed a man fall. Looking more closely she realised that the man was Donald and that two people were now helping him to his feet. She ran across to him and, to the astonishment of the small crowd gathering around Donald announced,

"This is my father. He's diabetic and he's 'hypo'. Once he's had something to eat he'll be fine."

At that moment a policeman arrived. Once Ruth had informed him of the situation he helped her take Donald to her car where she began to give him sugar. Meanwhile, the policeman found the Stirling bus and arranged for someone to collect Donald from Ruth's car. Donald was soon on the bus where he was plied with sweet tea, cakes and biscuits. Ruth drove home and phoned Peter who met the bus when it arrived in Stirling. The 'hypo' had been severe and Donald had not entirely recovered, so Peter drove him home.

If Ruth had not been in the right place at the right time, Donald would have been taken to hospital by ambulance and his friends in the Stirling bus would have searched for him in vain. Family and friends all agreed that Ruth's presence so close to Donald at the very moment he fell was a miracle, God's provision for his needs that evening.

Passionate for the gospel, Donald continued to be concerned about churches in Scotland. Since the early days of ministry in Bowmore, Donald had maintained his interest in island churches and had given support whenever he could. When it came to his attention that the Baptist churches in Islay were going through a difficult period and that the Baptist Union of Scotland was considering reducing the support given to them, Donald went to the Baptist Union officials personally. He passionately argued for the level of support to continue, because he knew from personal experience the unique difficulties and opportunities of island churches. His passion won the day and the churches were saved, combining resources under the name of Islay Baptist Church.

Another island church to benefit from Donald's ministry was the small Baptist Church in Bunessan, Isle of Mull. For many years it had not had a minister, relying on visiting preachers and its own members to provide ministry each Sunday. For a number of years Donald and Gwen had spent summer holidays in Mull and so they knew the local church and community well. They therefore readily agreed to go to Mull once a month during one winter to preach on the Sunday and also to visit people while they were there.

Throughout the years of retirement Donald kept up his contact with the Chinese Church in Glasgow, going regularly to speak at their meetings on a Sunday afternoon. They looked on him as a friend and pastor and he, in turn, loved to be with them, ministering to them by preaching at their services and being part of their lives. While in Adelaide Place Donald had baptised many of them and conducted many Chinese weddings. A number of these people had gone home to the Far East and wanted Donald and Gwen to visit them in their homes. They therefore very generously offered to pay all expenses if Donald and Gwen were able to go.

The pastor of the Chinese Church in Glasgow, Chi Ken Pan, began to make arrangements for Donald and Gwen to go to Singapore and Brunei and so in 1984 they set off to visit Chinese families who had once been part of the Adelaide Place congregation. First of all they went to Singapore where they stayed in a number of hotels. Most of their Chinese friends were working during the day, so Donald and Gwen were able to relax in the hotel or explore the area during the mornings and afternoons before meeting up with their friends in the evenings.

They enjoyed having time to visit Singapore's museums and the beautiful botanic gardens during the day as well as seeing many friends each evening.

Enjoying wonderful hospitality, they often went to people's homes for an evening meal but also were taken out to restaurants where they sampled the local food. Fish, a favourite meal, was always on the menu but Gwen was in for a surprise the first time she chose fish.

"There were huge tanks of fish, all swimming around. You had to pick the fish you wanted and then it was taken out to be cooked. It couldn't have been fresher!" she remarked.

She was also intrigued by the menu – baby pig, stuffed sea slugs, chicken roasted with prawn crackers, jelly inside little meat balls, shark fin soup, almond soup and even snake soup. Donald found that the food suited his needs very well, so he had no problem at all with his diabetes.

Apart from visiting friends, Donald took a large number of meetings during the holiday. This kept him quite busy, but he greatly appreciated the opportunity to minister to his friends once again. Always carefully prepared, he delivered a well received series of sermons to several different groups.

After some time in Singapore, Donald and Gwen took a flight to Brunei to stay with a Scottish girl who had married one of the men in the Glasgow Chinese Church and then moved out to the Far East. They had a beautiful home with a lovely garden where Donald and Gwen were able to relax, spending a good deal of time enjoying the sunshine and chatting before returning to Singapore for the flight home.

Once back in Scotland, Donald and Gwen settled back into their usual busy lifestyle. A particularly exciting event took place in October 1992 when Donald was invited to Granton Baptist Church to preach at the dedication of their new building. The church building which had been erected during Donald's ministry was no longer adequate for their needs, so the members had raised enough money to build an auditorium seating 350 people. Donald was delighted to see the new building opened and to take part in the dedication which followed. He was also astonished and humbled to realise that the old building, which was to become the church hall, was named after him – the McCallum Hall.

As Donald grew older he enjoyed reminiscing. Ever since serving in the Second World War, he had kept in touch with a number of his army friends, but until retirement he had not been able to spend much time with them. There were monthly meetings of the Normandy Veterans Association and once he retired Donald was free to attend. His army friend Alistair Armstrong regularly drove him to these meetings. It was not long before he became their padre, taking all the services at memorials as well as conducting services on Armistice Day in Glasgow, Paisley and Hamilton as well as one particularly memorable occasion when he preached at the Armistice Day service in the Church of the Holy Rude in Stirling. As the years went on Donald found more and more satisfaction in his role: taking services, giving pastoral help and wearing his medals with pride when on parade. He and his friends often thought about the men who had been killed or seriously injured during the war and marvelled that they had been spared.

Donald with some of his army friends at an Armistice Day service

As part of the Normandy Veterans Association, Donald and Gwen went to Normandy in 1989, the 45th anniversary of the landings and the liberation of Europe. Donald felt privileged to conduct a number of services, but also found the occasion a very sad one as he and his fellow veterans saw the graveyards which contained the bodies of so many men who did not come home. Before leaving, each veteran was presented with a special medal as a token of thanks from the people of France.

Donald and Gwen also went to Holland in October

1994 for the 51st Highland Division Reunion Pilgrimage. While there, they visited many of the villages the Division had liberated in 1944 and were greeted by ecstatic crowds, keen to give them a heroes' welcome and to show that they had never forgotten the sacrifice made by these men and their fellow soldiers. In the town of Vught they were taken on a tour of the town on World War Two vehicles, driving through crowds of cheering people. The men were also presented with a specially commissioned medal by the grateful townsfolk.

July 17th 1996 was a very special day for Donald and Gwen – the day they celebrated their golden wedding. Many friends rejoiced with them as they marked fifty years of very happy marriage. They had a quiet celebration on the day itself, but later in July they invited a large number of friends and relatives to a meal in Stirling Baptist Church, followed by a concert in one of the halls. It was a wonderful day with many people sharing their happiness. At the end of the meal Donald gave Gwen a surprise – he presented her with a medal for putting up with him for fifty years!

The month of August brought another important anniversary – fifty years of Christian ministry. Donald and Gwen celebrated quietly, but other people had different ideas and in the background plans were being made! First of all, the town of Stirling honoured Donald. He and Gwen were invited to a ceremony at Stirling Council's offices in Viewforth where Donald was presented with a symbolic key by the provost, John Paterson. Gwen was given a beautiful basket of flowers. This was a very happy occasion shared by some of the family who were able to be present.

The Central Baptist Association, which comprised the Baptist churches in central Scotland, wanted to celebrate the anniversary by giving Donald and Gwen a holiday to remember – a trip to the Holy Land. Without letting them know, they first of all asked Peter if Donald's health would be good enough for such a trip and then secretly asked churches to make donations. Peter Brown from the Denny church, who acted as treasurer, was delighted at the response from churches throughout Scotland. In reply he wrote:

"I have been overwhelmed by the response, which is evidence of the very high regard churches throughout Scotland have for these two lovely people."

The tour was arranged with Lifetime Christian Holidays and, thanks to the generosity of so many, enough money was raised to cover the cost of the trip and also provide some spending money.

Donald and Gwen were very grateful for such a generous gift and also extremely excited at the prospect of visiting the Holy Land. Donald had been in the Middle East during his army days, but for Gwen this was a completely new experience. After flying to London to join the rest of their party, their tour began on 26th November 1996. They were based in a hotel just north of Tel Aviv, from where they set out on five tours during the course of the holiday.

First of all they visited Emmaus and Bethlehem. The second tour took them to Caesarea and Nazareth, passing Mount Carmel, the Jezreel valley, Megiddo, Mount Tabor and Nain. A third tour took them to the River Jordan where some of the group were baptised, a sail on the Sea of Galilee, the town of Capernaum and the Mount of the Beatitudes. Next they visited the Judean Desert, the Mount of Temptation, Jericho, Qumran and the Dead Sea. The final tour allowed them to spend some time in Jerusalem, visiting the Mount of Olives, the Kidron Valley, the Garden of Gethsemane, the Upper Room, the Way of the Cross, the Temple area, the Western Wall, Caiphas' house and, finally, the Garden Tomb where they celebrated communion. This was a very busy schedule and at times Donald struggled to keep up with the pace, but he and Gwen loved it all. They both felt honoured and privileged to have such a memorable holiday, truly the trip of a lifetime.

During the years of retirement Donald and Gwen had a little more time to enjoy family life. In 1983 Donald returned to Adelaide Place to conduct Peter's marriage to Ann-Marie. Later on Peter and Ann-Marie moved from Glasgow to Stirling, so they were able to see much more of them.

Gwen took great pleasure in spending days with Ruth's family, taking the bus from Kippen to Glasgow in the morning and returning home in the evening, while they both enjoyed the times when Charles, Ruth and family visited Kippen. Occasionally the children stayed overnight, loving the little bedroom upstairs in the attic and being thoroughly spoiled by Gwen!

As the three grand-children grew up, Donald was delighted when they all made Christian commitments and he had the great pleasure of baptising two of them – Donald and Kirsty. He was particularly proud of Kirsty when she took a year out after completing her degree and joined a BMS (Baptist Missionary Society) Action Team, going to work with a church in one of the favelas in Sao Paulo, Brazil.

Over the years of retirement Donald's health gave increasing cause for concern. On a number of occasions he was admitted to Stirling Royal Infirmary and he worried about Gwen driving from Kippen into Stirling to see him. In 1998 the decision was made to move into Stirling where they would be nearer the hospital and so, after looking at a number of properties, they sold their lovely cottage in Kippen and in November of that year moved to Cambusbarron, on the outskirts of Stirling. The house in Cambusbarron did not have the charm of the little cottage in Kippen, but it suited their needs.

Inevitably, Donald's health continued to deteriorate as fifty years of diabetes caught up with him. The medical staff who dealt with him were continually amazed at the way he had coped so well with his condition for so long, exclaiming in disbelief when he told them how long he had been diabetic. He always gave Gwen the credit, knowing that only her loving care over so many years had kept him in reasonably good health.

In the autumn of 2000, Donald and Gwen enjoyed a lovely holiday in Bowmore, meeting friends and enjoying a stay in the Bowmore manse, much changed from their days there but nevertheless a reminder of their happy years in the village. Donald felt privileged to preach in the church on the Sunday. However, soon after their return to Stirling Donald became very unwell and was admitted to hospital on several occasions over the next few months. In spite of illness he was determined to keep going to church as often as possible, particularly on one Sunday in January 2001.

It was a snowy morning and Donald was barely well enough to go out, but he was due to take part in the morning service at Stirling Baptist Church. Church members had run a café in the approach to Christmas 2000, raising money for several good causes. One of these causes was close to Donald's heart – the Elpis Centre which he had been instrumental in founding while in Glasgow – and Donald was to present the cheque to its manager. He was so determined to go that he rose at 4am to ensure that he would be ready in time. Peter, knowing how little energy Donald had for even the ordinary events of everyday life, went to the house to help him get ready and then drove Donald and Gwen to church before setting off for his own day's work as a bus driver. Donald was therefore able to present the cheque and before doing so he spoke movingly about the work of Elpis over the years. Unfortunately he did not feel well enough to stay for the whole service, but in spite of ill health his enthusiasm for the gospel was undimmed.

As winter gave way to spring, Donald's health continued to deteriorate and eventually he was admitted to the Strathcarron Hospice in Denny where he had been chaplain at the beginning of his retirement. The staff at the hospice were wonderful, improving his condition to the point where he was able to return home for a few weeks before being re-admitted. Gwen greatly appreciated the love and care shown to Donald and to herself at this difficult time.

Soon after his return to the hospice Donald's childhood friend, Jack Carr, died. Donald and he had remained close friends over the years, both serving the Baptist Union of Scotland with distinction. For many years Jack and his wife, Gertrude, had lived in Dunblane and so they had been able to keep up their friendship. In spite of being seriously ill himself, Donald was determined to go to Jack's funeral and deliver an appreciation. Convinced that he could not write a speech in the hospice, he persuaded the staff to allow him home once again for a few days where he spent time in his study composing the speech before giving it to Ruth to type up for him. On the day of Jack's funeral, however, he was so ill that he had to return to the hospice, but his speech was read out to the congregation.

After giving tribute to Jack and to the family connections which had been so strong, Donald's speech continued:

"Now Jack has gone home to the Father's house. No-one is afraid to go home, there is nowhere like home, and no home like the Father's house where there are many resting places, and Jack has arrived there."

Two days later, on the morning of Sunday 8th July 2001, Donald went home too. Many family members had visited him over the last few days and Gwen and Ruth were beside him when he died. The funeral on the following Thursday in Stirling Baptist Church was well attended, with many friends from far and wide coming to pay their last respects. Donald was laid to rest in Kippen cemetery. Members of the Veterans Association marched from the cemetery gate to the graveside and then played a recording of 'The Last Post' - a very moving ceremony, and one which would have pleased Donald immensely.

Donald had often been amazed at what God had done with an ordinary wee boy from Edinburgh, but the secret of his life is made clear in the headstone which Gwen had erected later that year. On it is a quotation from the Bible, from 1 Kings chapter 14 verse 8, words which give an accurate picture of Donald's life:

"He followed God with all his heart."

Over the next few weeks and months Gwen received dozens of letters, cards and phone-calls, showing how much Donald had been loved. She treasured all of these as she had to settle down to a very different life. There were, however, two very pleasant surprises to come. One of these came about when Stirling Baptist Church refurbished its halls and decided to name two of the halls after previous ministers, one of whom was Donald. Gwen was therefore invited to cut the ribbon at the opening of the new hall and to name it 'The McCallum Room'. This brought her very great pleasure.

The second surprise came in October 2005 when Gwen received a phone call from the minister of Islay Baptist Church who was in Stirling at the assembly meetings of the Baptist Union of Scotland and wanted to visit Gwen in order to give her information about an award which was to be presented in Donald's name. Baptists in Islay had long been grateful for Donald's ministry from 1946 to 1950 and for his continuing support of their church, from the day he left the island in 1950 until his death over fifty years later. Now they had the opportunity to demonstrate their thanks in a tangible way.

Islay Baptist Church, in conjunction with their partner church, Calvary Baptist Church in Baltimore USA, was going to present the Rev. Donald P. McCallum Memorial Shield which would be given each year at Islay High School to the pupil who best showed the qualities of endeavour and commitment, qualities which Donald had had in abundance. The pupil gaining the award would also be given the opportunity to spend two weeks in the USA as a guest of the Baltimore church.

Gwen was thrilled at this unexpected honour and at the invitation to present the shield in person. Ruth and Peter were determined that she should go to Bowmore for the occasion so Peter agreed to take her there and they rented a cottage for a few days, setting off for Islay in the last week of June 2006. The days were full and satisfying – meals with friends, a tour of the High School, appreciation of the lovely countryside as they drove around, all leading up to the climax when Gwen presented the shield at the Islay High School prize giving.

All too soon it was time to go home. As the ferry pulled out of Port Askaig, Gwen looked again with pleasure at the scene she knew so well. She rejoiced in God's goodness over many years and gave thanks for the incredible years with Donald, that "ordinary wee boy from Edinburgh".

About the Author

Ruth Millican is Donald McCallum's daughter. She and her husband live near Glasgow and have three grown-up children and one grandchild. Ruth teaches English in a school on the outskirts of Glasgow. She graduated MA at Edinburgh University before going into teaching. During her teaching career she has obtained a Diploma in Support for Learning as well as a Masters Degree in Education.

Lightning Source UK Ltd.
Milton Keynes UK
UKHW010623180721
387337UK00001B/19